The goddess

To my Mother

The goddess

Myths and Stories

Lindel Barker-Revell

SMITHMARK

This edition published in 1999 by SMITHMARK Publishers,
a division of U.S. Media Holdings, Inc.,
115 West 18th Street, New York, NY 10011

SMITHMARK books are available for bulk purchase for sales
promotion and premium use. For details write or call the manager of
special sales, SMITHMARK Publishers
115 West 18th Street, New York, NY 10011

Produced by
Lansdowne Publishing Pty Ltd, Sydney
First published in 1997

ISBN 0-7651-1025-3

Printed in Hong Kong by South China Printing

10 9 8 7 6 5 4 3 2 1

Library of Congress Catalog Card Number: 98-75031

Front cover: DIANA THE HUNTER, *Orazio Gentileschi
(1565–1647)*

ABOUT THE AUTHOR

Lindel Barker-Revell

Lindel Barker-Revell is a writer and games inventor. She has a Masters degree in Applied Science (Social Ecology); her studies focused on feminism, ancient mythology and myths emerging in our time. An educator for over 20 years, Lindel has now turned her attention to writing.

Always interested in the esoteric traditions, Lindel has practiced astrology for 17 years and the mystical Tarot for 23 years. In 1989 she co-invented the astrological boardgame, *Revelation: The Game of the Future*. Her first book *The Tarot and You* was published in 1995.

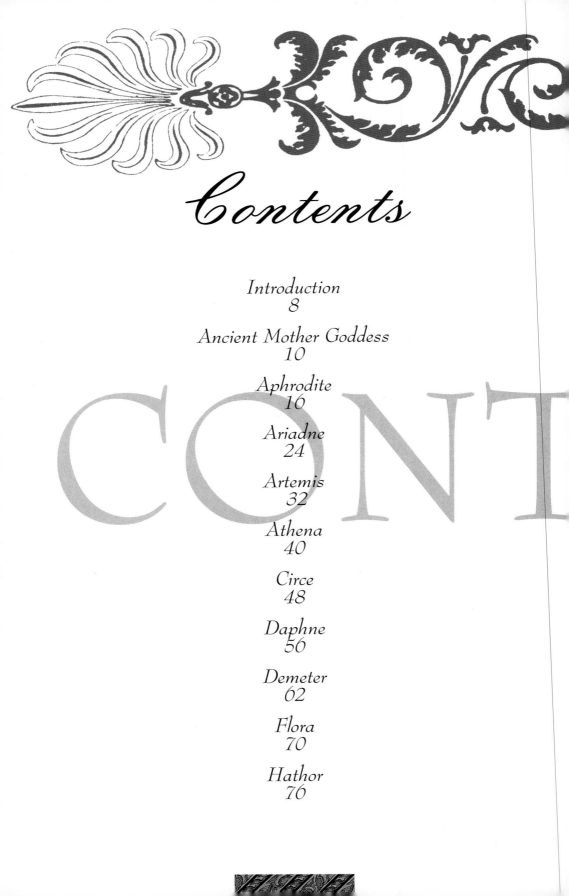

Contents

Introduction

L ove of story unites all humans, and myths are the richest stories in the world. The language and imagery of myth is so powerful and immediate, it reaches through thousands of years to entertain and astonish us today. Myths are folk stories involving the activities of gods and ordinary humans, generally placed in a non-historical setting. While on the surface myths are merely "the telling of tales", they have a deeper level that reveals profound truths of human and godly existence, especially of the relationship of human to god or goddess, and conversely of god to human. Homer and Hesiod recorded the myths of the Greeks between 900–700 BC, but these myths were already very ancient. These spiritually potent stories were told orally, in some cases for thousands of years, before they were written down.

Myths reveal to us what was important to earlier peoples. The cow was so significant to the survival of the ancient Egyptians, the heavens were personified as the goddess Hathor, Cow of Heaven. Many myths of earlier peoples reflect their dependence on agriculture and the cycle of the seasons.

When ancient humans looked at their world they asked the universal questions. Who made the world? How will the world end? Where do we go after we die? Why do we have winter? Where does the sun go at night? The answers are the stuff of myth. Whatever happens in the mythic world mirrors life in the culture which has given birth to that myth. The ancient Greeks, known also as Hellenes, had inquiring minds and created stories to answer their great questions. These myths are our Western heritage, the inspiration for our poetry, plays, music and the visual arts.

Legends differ from myths in that legends relate the exploits of supposed historical figures. An example of such a legend is the story of the mortal woman Miao Shan who becomes the goddess Kuan Yin.

Seemingly diverse cultures have the Goddess hidden deeply beneath the mythlogy. Generally, the earlier the source of the myth, the more powerful is the sense of the Goddess. As cultures change, and invasions or migrations take place, new myths are laid over the top of earlier myths, always attempting to show the invader as stronger, or better suited to rule. So, when reading a Greek myth about a goddess, we are reading a story formulated from a male perspective laid over the myth from earlier times when the Goddess was more revered. This change occurred around 2500 BC when Aryan invaders came from the north through India, Europe and the Mediterranean. The cultural and religious systems in all those countries were transformed from goddess worshiping, agricultural peoples to systems based on sky god worship and male supremacy. Hence many Greek myths describe rape or the powerlessness of women — this theme is well illustrated in the myths surrounding Leda and Daphne. In Indian myth, although the gods are powerful and numerous, the Goddess is seen as the sacred place from which all the gods arise.

Different versions of myths abound; the stories in this volume are my interpretation of the myths of several cultures.

I studied both ancient sources and more modern re-tellings in order to create the sense of the Goddess emerging from within and beneath the myths of history. The images of myth are like the dream images of an individual dreamer; they linger and are not forgotten, yet are not easily remembered in full. However, beneath the veneer of mythology lies the Goddess, slumbering, but not dead. She fascinates, from a place unvisited, a time unknown; yet we feel her fears and joys and sense her power.

Ancient Mother Goddess

Images of the Mother Goddess are powerful. They seem to reach out from the past to catch our attention. To put the Goddess into perspective we must look back to Paleolithic times where she was the unifying principle underlying religion and all life. Early Paleolithic times date back to about 600 000 years BC, lasting until the Mesolithic era which began around 8000 BC. About 100 000 years ago the first Neanderthal humans emerged.

We judge a civilization not only by what it did or thought and wrote, but also by what it made. As well as the implements left by the ancient ones, there have been discoveries of almost one hundred thousand images of Mother Goddesses. Dating from around 33 000 BC–9000 BC

Left: Anatolian mother goddess giving birth, Catal-Hüyük, c. 6000–5800 BC.

Opposite: Sumerian earth goddess in terracotta and lime, 2000 BC.

such sacred images of goddesses appeared from the Pyrenees to Siberia. Mother Goddess figures are not like ordinary women, but are images of the creative force within woman which brings forth and nourishes life. Crafted in stone, bone, and ivory, all the figures are naked, often pregnant, and sometimes in the process of giving birth. They have large milk-filled breasts and huge stomachs, as if to emphasize the life-giving aspect of woman. Sometimes the breasts and buttocks of the statues appear like four great eggs, carried within the body.

These statues were often small enough to hold in the hand and were tapered to a point; many of the figures were found embedded in the earth, standing upright. Such places would have been consecrated places for worship or ritual.

At first, these figurines were dismissively called "fert-ility symbols", but the number of the sculptures and the geographic extent of their locations point to something more. The goddess images appear to be the religious symbols of a people who worshiped a Mother Goddess. Paleolithic peoples perhaps viewed themselves as children of Mother Nature. They certainly revered the female form, in giving birth, offering the breast, and in receiving the dead back into the earth. Fewer images of male counterparts were found.

Around 4500–2500 BC there was a gradual transformation of images as power moved from female to male in much of Europe, though goddesses were still found in the civilizations of Crete and in some parts of the Mediterranean and the Aegean.

The Goddess of Willendorf (Austria) is approximately 30 000 years old and was originally carved from limestone. It is the oldest sculpture of the human body yet discovered. Only 4⅓ inches (11 cm) tall, yet she seems massive, and her form suggests abundant life. She gazes down at the fullness of her own breasts and stomach, as if contemplating what may possibly come into being. Her head is notched with seven rows of indentations. Perhaps these represent the seven moving planets visible to the naked eye. One quarter of the moon's full cycle is seven days. It is interesting that these symbols are found on the head, possibly indicating matters on which to ponder.

In the times when the Great Mother was worshiped, humans lived in harmony with their environment. Such cultures revered the earth and saw themselves as part of nature — they were not apart from it, nor did they have dominion over it. The most ancient forms of the Goddess depict her as being clearly linked to animals, birds and the natural world. She is seen as fish, snake and bird goddess, often guarded by lionesses or other large cats. Important motifs which create a kind of symbolic language of the

Left: The Venus of Willendorf.
30 000–25 000 BC.

Goddess are intersecting spirals suggesting the interconn-
ectedness of the generations, and "V"s and triangles, which
suggest the pubic triangle. Also found on or near the figures
are inscriptions of rhthmic, waving lines, serpentine shapes
and butterflies and bees, which seem to suggest the
connection of earth and air, life and death.

Similar symbols reappeared in the murals and artworks of
Crete, a much later civilization which revered the Goddess as
central to all life.

In myth and art, the Mother Goddess was always
associated with the three phases of the moon. Ancient
carvings in stone show the Goddess holding the crescent
moon, or she appears with notches carved alongside her,
indicating the twenty eight days of the lunar month and the
menstrual cycle. These phases of the moon represent the life
cycle of woman; the slipper of the crescent
moon may be imagined as the Maiden or
Virgin; the full moon as the Mother, full
of life; and the dark moon as the Wise
One, or Crone, no longer fertile, withering
away in order to be born again.

The Goddess often has these
three "faces" in myth, just as the
virgin Artemis appears also as
Selene the Mother and as Hecate
the Crone. Artemis is some-times
pictured with three heads to show her
triple aspect.

When the Great Mother
Goddess reigned she was sup-
reme, immortal and omnipotent.
She presided over birth, life and

*Right: Grey terracotta Mother Goddess
from Mathura, India.*

death, and all the natural rhythms, seen and unseen. She ruled the heavens, the earth and sea, and the underworld or afterlife for it was she who received the dead back into her body. The Great Mother was given many names: Queen of Heaven, Lady of the Animals, Ruler of the Underworld, Giver of Numbers, Corn Mother, Rice Mother, Keeper of Pleasure, Lady of the Land, Queen of the Cosmos, Green One, Queen of the Dead, Mother-of-All, Queen of Celestial Light, Seed-Producer, Keeper of the Dark Crossroads. In various incarnations she was called "She of the Thousand Names". Some of these names live on in our modern religions; but divorced from the reverence and interconnection of all life, her names exist in fragments, here and there. Wholeness was lost when she became divided by the Greeks into four or five goddesses, each expressing just one of her many qualities: Aphrodite as lover, Demeter as mother, Artemis as virgin, Athena as wisdom, Hera as wife.

The images of the ancient Mother Goddess can connect us to transformational concepts of the feminine, where woman is revered. Deeply buried, but not lost, are ideas of the neverending rotations of birth, life and death, and respect for the cycles of nature in its strength and its fragility. Her way is the way of interdependence with nature and other human beings. Her way is one of power with, rather than dominion over, the rest of life.

Left: Crowned snake goddess from Crete, Neolithic period, c.4500 BC.

Right: Terracotta relief of Lilith/Inanna/Ishtar as a bird goddess, Mesopotamia, c.2300 BC.

14

Aphrodite

Greece

Aphrodite, goddess of love, is perhaps the best known of the Greek goddesses. In her Roman form she is known as Venus. Aphrodite, the "White Bird of Heaven" came to Greece from Cyprus, and before that from ancient Mesopotamia. Aphrodite means "born of the foam", but airborne doves, swans and geese were her constant companions.

Aphrodite reveals her ancient descent by her water birth, the place where all life begins, and by her accompanying birds, for from Palaeolithic times, the bird was one of the earliest images of the goddess. Aphrodite was probably brought by sea-traders to the islands off Greece as one of the Great Mother goddesses of the eastern Mediterranean. Many scholars agree Aphrodite comes from the earlier mythologies of Sumeria and Babylon, where her ancestors were Inanna and Ishtar whose stories date from c.5000 BC. The following myth, however, comes from the Greek poet Homer, c.900 BC.

Greek mythology diminished Aphrodite to a goddess of love, passion and jealousy — in their older forms, goddesses never had just one area of sovereignty, they encompassed all areas of human life, especially life and death. In her swan drawn carriage or riding a goose, Aphrodite was the original Mother Goose. However the myths and stories about Aphrodite reflect the area of life the Greeks attributed to her — love. Her star was the morning and evening star which we call by her Roman name, Venus. The word aphrodisiac reminds us of Aphrodite, when even today certain seafoods are consumed for their passion inducing properties.

Right: Greek terracotta statue of Aphrodite riding on a swan and carrying a casket, an ancient goddess symbol, c.480 BC.

MYTHS OF APHRODITE

The Birth of Aphrodite

In ancient days during the battle for supremacy in the heavens, Cronos attacked his father Uranus with a stone sickle. He severed Uranus's genitals which he tossed into the ocean. For a long time they were thrown about on the wild sea until white foam gathered around them. From this foam was born an immortal maiden named Aphrodite who, having taken form, began to swim in the vast waters. Delighting in the shape of her new body she swam until she came to the shores of the island of Cyprus. There she stepped from the waves, and where she walked upon the earth, grass sprouted sweet and green beneath her feet.

Cyprus was the home of the Horai, or Seasons, daughters of Themis, goddess of natural law and justice and of the correct relations between the sexes. The Horai greeted Aphrodite, who shimmered with golden light as she emerged from the foaming waves.

"Hail Aphrodite, Golden One," they said, watching her shake what looked like foam-covered feathers. "Hail, Queen of the waters, the earth and the air."

As they spoke, Aphrodite seemed to swiftly change before their eyes. Now she was riding a dolphin, now driving her chariot drawn by swans, now riding astride a great goose. Then she appeared as Lady of the Animals, surrounded by all the animals of the earth. An aura of love pervaded the animals and they drew off quietly in twos and lay down together in affection. The Horai had seen many things in their lives, but before the glory of Aphrodite they knelt and offered her garments they had created and sandals for her divine feet.

When clothed, Aphrodite was brought among the gods who embraced and kissed her, each desiring to wed her.

Right: APHRODITE, *Briton Riviero (1840–1920).*

Because of her extraordinary beauty and ability to inspire the passion of love and lust in gods and men, Aphrodite was given dominion over these realms. She wore a magic girdle which would disarm any man or god who threatened her.

Humans who desired love made offerings to Aphrodite in the temples and shrines which sprang up all over Greece. For Aphrodite blessed love in all its forms, whether godly, animal or human, or the blossoming of flower or tree. From the power of love, Aphrodite inspired the creativity of life and gave joyful self-expression to those who sought her. On the island of Cythera a sculptor, in a frenzy of admiration and desire, created the first naked image of Aphrodite. The statue was so beautiful that it inspired artists forever after to seek to capture the elusive qualities of the goddess of love. And Aphrodite remained the only Greek goddess who was ever portrayed naked before her people.

Left: Aphrodite, the 'Venus de Milo', Hellenistic. c.100 BC.

Aphrodite and Adonis

One important story of Aphrodite was that of her love for Adonis, whose name means *Lord*, for of all her many admirers, Aphrodite loved him best.

Magically born from the myrrh tree, Adonis was dedicated by his mother to Aphrodite, who upon seeing the beautiful baby, fell in love with him. Placing him gently in a chest she took him to Persephone (Proserpina is her Roman name), queen of the underworld, for safe-keeping. When Persephone opened the chest and saw Adonis, she too fell in love with the baby, and refused ever to part with him. Aphrodite, mad with grief, threatened to spread her loving energies no more upon the heavens and the earth.

Above: Greek terracotta plaque fragment depicting Aphrodite riding on a swan's back, c.460-450 BC.

Above: VENUS AND HER NYMPHS, *Ebenezer Wake Cook (1843–1926).*

Zeus came to settle the dispute between the two goddesses. He adjudicated that Adonis would spend part of the year in the underworld with Persephone while winter was upon the land, and the rest of the year in the sunshine with Aphrodite. Until Adonis grew to manhood he could live with Aphrodite on earth. The goddesses accepted the wise ruling, as it was in accordance with the ancient lore of vegetation which could not be questioned.

Adonis grew into the beautiful young man that his birth had promised. Aphrodite loved him and watched over him like the most protective of mothers. One day Adonis was seized by

the desire to go hunting, although Aphrodite had warned him never to go alone into the woods. There Adonis met his destiny when he was attacked by a wild boar which gored him almost to death. From far off Aphrodite heard his moans. With a feeling of dreadful foreboding she mounted her swan-drawn carriage. With all haste she followed the sounds, but when she reached the place, Adonis lay dead in a pool of blood.

"Oh my Lord, my love," Aphrodite said, and wept. "It is come, the time for you to leave me." She moaned as she rocked the still warm body of Adonis. "So short is the time of love."

Sensing the impatient Persephone below her, Aphrodite allowed the earth to open and carry Adonis, outstretched, to the world below. She touched the place where his blood lay spilt, and among the roots of an ancient olive tree, beside the sweet wild hyacinths, sprang the first, black-hearted, red anemone.

"You, flower, will be short-lived, like love. Your petals will be blown open by the wind, and by that same wind will they be blown away leaving your dark heart to grieve." Thus spoke Aphrodite to the red anemone, which grows even now on that hillside in spring, and is known to the people thereabouts as the "wind flower".

In this way Aphrodite yearly suffered the greatest of pain to all lovers, separation from her beloved. Adonis would die each year and enter the underworld so the earth could lie fallow and rest until the spring flowers heralded his return.

Ariadne

Crete – Greece

Ariadne's myth describes a goddess and a culture in transition. As Mycenaean migrants from mainland Greece settled in Crete after a series of massive earthquakes around 1450 BC, the stable goddess worshiping culture of Crete became disordered. Faith in the old ways was literally shaken by the earthquakes, and Crete was vulnerable to penetration by new ideas. The migrants from Mycenae brought their culture and their myths. They in turn absorbed some of the fascinating, creative mystery of Cretan culture into their own. Ariadne was one such goddess who made the transition.

Early Cretan culture (from about 3000 BC to 1100 BC) was called Minoan, after King Minos and the cult of the bull. A highly sophisticated culture, Crete displayed spirited, joyful arts including dance and poetry as well as fine, unfortified architecture and excellent plumbing with indoor running water in the towns. All this in an atmosphere of peace and equality between the sexes. The Greeks' admiration for the Minoan culture was so profound that they attributed the place of birth for most of their gods and goddesses to Crete; it was also the site for many of the immortals' important times.

Before Ariadne came into Greek myth, she was the great Minoan moon goddess, "Mother of All". The Minoan culture left no writing, so we can only guess at her exact role. Perhaps Ariadne was originally a vegetation goddess worshiped only by women and had sovereignty over the cycles of the seasons.

This story of Ariadne was told by the Greek poet Homer in the Odyssey (c.900 BC) and Plutarch (c.80 AD) but contains much earlier Cretan elements (c.3000 BC)

Above: MINOTAUR, *George Frederick Watts (1817–1904).*

MYTH OF ARIADNE

On the fertile island of Crete, Minos was king and Ariadne was his daughter. Together they sat watching the harbor, Ariadne suffering anxiety. For some days now, they had been waiting for signs of the ship bringing fourteen young Athenians to Crete. These young people, seven maidens and seven youths, were to be fed to the Minotaur, the half-man, half-bull, who lived beneath the palace. Even now he raged and bellowed, as he paced the serpentine labyrinth, ravenous for human flesh.

Some years before, King Minos had defeated the Athenians in a great sea battle. He had exacted the tribute that each year Athens must contribute food for the Minotaur, in the form of living human flesh. King Minos had also promised that should any brave youth kill the beast, the tribute would cease and the Athenians could return home.

Above: THESEUS WITH ARIADNE AND PHAEDRA, THE DAUGHTERS OF KING MINOS, *Benedetto Gennari the Younger (1633–1715).*

Recently Ariadne began to feel a stirring within her, a feeling of imminent change. She had been waking in great fear from dark dreams. Ariadne's normal ability to read prophecies and omens seemed lost, and she felt almost as if a fog were beginning to envelop her. No matter how hard she tried, she could not push away the sense that her destiny was drawing near. Restlessly, she watched for the ship from her room, listening to the Minotaur in the caverns deep below.

Theseus, prince of Athens, sailed to Crete in a boat with black sails. On this ship all feared for their fate. Theseus, had

sworn to his father, King Aegus, that he would kill the monster and bring the young Athenians back safely, or die in the attempt. Theseus embraced his father saying:

"Watch for my ship. I will hoist white sails to show you I have been successful. Do not fear father, I will return."

King Aegus had let the salty tears dry on his cheeks as he watched the ship until it was a dark dot on the horizon. When Theseus's band arrived in Crete, they paraded past the waiting crowd. The people stood silently, honoring the sacrificial victims, grateful that young Cretans no longer needed to be sent as living food for the Minotaur.

Ariadne watched the approaching band, her senses alert, her skin prickling. In the moment her eyes lit upon Theseus, Ariadne's heart leapt. She was so unexpectedly transported by deep feelings that she felt pain as well as pleasure. How handsome he was. The curl of his hair on his strong brown neck seemed intimately known to her, yet he was a stranger. Surely this man could not carry her destiny. Suddenly Theseus glanced at Ariadne, held her gaze and she received the full impact of his brown eyes. Her breath felt hot in her mouth and a strange buzzing reverberated in her ears. On the decorated walls of the buildings of Crete, the butterflies and sacred bees alone observed the meeting of Ariadne and Theseus.

As their eyes held, he smiled. He was on the way to his probable death yet he was as full of beauty as a spirited young animal. Ariadne resolved to help him. She ran to her chamber and picked up a ball of spun yarn, which she hid in her gown. She knew the labyrinth better than any except its creator, and with this knowledge she resolved to aid the foreigner, the man whose smile had entered her heart. With all haste she ran to the compound where the victims were waiting before the doorway into the labyrinth. Ariadne stole close to where Theseus was standing, his head held high.

"Take this thread," she whispered, slipping it into his hand. "When you enter the labyrinth, secure an end near the doorway.

Above: ARIADNE AT NAXOS, *Evelyn de Morgan (1855–1919).*

Let the thread unravel as you go. You will then be able to find your way out."

Theseus smiled at the beautiful young woman who stood beside him. "Wait for me. I will take you with me to Athens," he said. "For I love you already, though I don't even know your name."

Ariadne told him and slipped away, her heart and mind racing. What am I doing? Why is love such a tumult? Why is my destiny taking me in such a direction? Her thoughts tumbled one after another. Behind her she heard the clang of the labyrinth door slamming shut behind the fourteen young Athenians.

In the labyrinth, Theseus fulfilled his promise to his father. With bare hands he fell upon the Minotaur and after a fierce struggle killed it. Using Ariadne's thread Theseus found his way out of the maze of twists and turns and joined his

anxious friends. Rejoicing they cried: "The Minotaur is dead! The monster is defeated!" and were set free by the astonished attendants.

After victoriously parading before the Cretans they set sail for Athens. Beside Theseus stood the cloaked Ariadne, her beautiful face flushed with emotion as she watched her homeland diminish in size until it disappeared into the blue waters of the ocean.

Resting overnight on the island of Naxos, Theseus lay with Ariadne on a simple bed made of cloaks flung across the soft sands near the shore. Before dawn Theseus awoke and called to the others to prepare to sail, for he wanted to make haste, the sooner to arrive in Athens and tell his father the good news. Strange as it may seem, Theseus forgot his bride completely, so that when Ariadne awoke she was alone.

Later, Theseus blamed the goddess Athena, saying that she had put upon him the sleep of forgetfulness. Theseus also forgot to raise the white sails as they approached the coast at Attica. King Aegus, still awaiting his beloved son, saw the black sails and with a howl of grief, flung himself from the cliff and died. In this sad way did Theseus become King of Athens.

But what of Ariadne? Some say that Ariadne, upon waking and realizing she had been abandoned, hanged herself from a stark tree on the cliff top. Many storytellers describe the following outcome.

Ariadne awoke, put her head in her hands and wept for her beloved Crete, where she had reigned as priestess of the moon. Her name had meant "Most Holy", and she had led the women of Crete into the sacred mysteries of womanhood. Ariadne grieved for her forsaken brother, the Minotaur, who as the sacred man-bull had been revered in ancient days. Ariadne cried for her past, which seemed to be dissolving in her mind, as though the sacred feminine truths she knew were being forgotten with her, on the rocky island of Naxos.

Above: BACCHUS AND ARIADNE, *Charles Joseph Natoire (1700–1777).*

A long time she grieved alone, when a merry band approached her. Naxos was the favorite haunt of the god Dionysus (Bacchus) and his followers, and that very day they were dancing along the shore, looking for somewhere to feast and continue their revelry. When Dionysus saw Ariadne, lamenting on the beach he fell in love with her. He immediately presented himself to her, and with great flourish, bowed low and asked her to marry him. Dionysus had been born on Crete and was well known to Ariadne. Suddenly understanding that Dionysus, not Theseus, was her destiny, she took his hand and made an ancient Cretan gesture of the Goddess accepting the God. A great cycle of her existence had ended as she left Crete, and Theseus had been the instrument of her fate, for here before her was the one god she could love.

Dionysus gave to his bride the wedding gift of a golden

Right: Ariadne receiving her betrothal gifts from Dionysus (Bacchus). BACCHUS AND ARIADNE, *Sebastiano Ricci (1658–1734).*

crown, shining with seven sparkling gems. He consoled Ariadne, loved her, and made her an unaging goddess. Dionysus was ever faithful to her, and together they had three children. Ariadne, for her part, stayed by his side, and when she wearied of earthly life Dionysus raised her to heaven, to sparkle as the seven stars in her crown which even now twinkle as the constellation between the kneeling Hercules and the Holder of the Serpent.

Artemis

Greece

In modern times when most of us live in cities Artemis, known in her Roman form as Diana, can remind us of the wild, untamed face of ourselves and the Goddess. Like Isis from Egypt, Artemis had many names and was worshiped in many ancient countries. In Western art Artemis is depicted as the huntress, the guardian of animals and guardian of her own virginity. The Many Breasted Artemis of Ephesus is a powerful fertility symbol indicating the links between Artemis and the ancient Great Mother Goddess who nurtured the living. Her temple at Ephesus from the fourth century BC is one of the Seven Wonders of the World. In the following myth Artemis is shown in her virgin form, but it is important to remember that she is the triple goddess of old. The name Artemis has no certain meaning in any language, but is rather an amalgam of names, just as Artemis the goddess seems to be the mergence of different divinities.

Artemis is the Lady of the Wild Things, and she has become synonymous with wilderness itself. She is the tree, the mountain, the bear, the wolf and the rabbit. She is also the personification of natural law, and can be ferocious as well as nurturing. Artemis will fiercely protect all that is wild and vulnerable.

Right: Marble statue of Artemis from Ephesus as goddess of fertility with many breasts, 2nd century.

Above: DIANA THE HUNTER, *Orazio Gentileschi (1565-1647).*

MYTH OF ARTEMIS

When Artemis was born it is said that her joyous mother Leto suffered no labor pains. Artemis then assisted her mother for nine long days as she struggled to give birth to Apollo. As she lay exhausted, Leto looked at her two divine children and named Artemis, goddess of the moon, and Apollo, god of the sun.

"You, my daughter, will be called upon by women and all she-creatures in the time of birthing, for you have the divine gift of healing and guiding the birth pains." She looked at her brilliant-eyed son, his hair a corona of gold. "And you, my son, will have many gifts and will always shine as brightly as the sun."

By a powerful premonition, Leto knew that neither of her children would find true love. Pushing the knowledge aside, she smiled at Artemis who, in the way of divine children, was already fully grown. "Dear Artemis, you will remain wild. No god or man will tame you, for there is a wildness in your soul."

The twins grew up as different in temperament as the day is from night. Artemis, shy as the slipper moon, approached her father Zeus (Jupiter) for a gift. "All I want is a hunting tunic, a bow, a quiver full of arrows," she said. Her father much amused, granted her request. Artemis stood still before him, girlish yet strong in her new clothing. "There is something more, my father," she said. He raised a dark eyebrow in question. "I beg you give me the gift of eternal virginity," Artemis said with conviction. Zeus, amused, yet sensing some ancient reason for her request, decreed it should be so. Thus Artemis left Mount Olympus for deeply wooded Arcadia in her desire to roam free.

Running wild in the forest was life to Artemis. With wolf and bear, stag and lion, she ran. Hers was the way of the wilderness, deep and mysterious. She hunted the animals she also protected, and kept them not as pets, but as equals in the wild places of the heart. Every tree was known to Artemis, she

Above: DIANA AND HER FOLLOWERS, LUNATICS (WORSHIPPERS OF THE MOON), *Christine de Pisan (c. 1364–1430).*

learnt the scent of every new herb which burst into flower. She knew the language of the streams and rivers and every creature in her domain.

The nymphs and priestesses who begged to learn her tough, outdoor ways had to take the same pledge she had given her father, eternal chastity. "You belong to yourself!"

Artemis would say vehemently. "No one man is your master. Promise this." And the nymphs would vow, and receive the gift of the sacred bow and arrow. Little by little the nymphs learned the craft of survival in the wild Arcadian forests, the craggy mountains, the dark caverns and the wet woods. They learned the rules of the hunt and the chase which Artemis taught them according to her ancient memories. They became raw, wild women, who lived roughly in the forests, hunting and learning the ways of the land.

At certain phases of the moon, Artemis would tell stories of how she had come from far away in Crete. When the moon was full she would tell of herself as mother to all nature, and how she would bring swift retribution on any Greek who pursued a pregnant animal, or those with young — as they all knew, such creatures were especially protected by Artemis.

When the moon was new and all that could be seen was a glimmer by firelight, Artemis would tell of when she had lived in Anatolia and was called wise Hecate, She of the Crossroads. The newly arrived nine year old nymphs would sit round eyed as Artemis told the stories, hugging their knees, their breath coming in light, short gasps.

"I will tell of the time a hunter called Actaeon disobeyed my ruling that none should look upon my nakedness," Artemis said into the firelight. "It was long ago now, though it seems just a breath ago in time. I was undertaking my bathing ritual in the sea, where the waves pound loudly on the rocks. I did not notice that Actaeon and his hounds had taken rest not far above where I was washing, but after a while I felt a warning, prickling in the back of my neck. A knowledge came to me that all was not as it should be.

When I turned and beheld the man's face observing me with a look of such lasciviousness, a rage struck deep into my heart. In that moment I turned that watcher into a stag, and myself into a swift-footed hound."

Left: Marble sculpture of Hecate and Artemis, as part of the triple goddess, Attic period, 3rd century.

The hush around the camp fire was almost palpable. Artemis continued softly, but her mouth had taken upon it a look of the sharp muzzle of a hunting dog, and her voice seemed to come in a deep growl. "I leapt towards him, gathering his own hounds as I went, for they had been dozing in the shade. They saw the stag and took flight with me as we gave chase. We followed him a good way through many a glade and over three hills. I stepped back as we cornered him, and ..." Her eyes gleamed blood red in the dying light of the fire. "I watched as his own hounds tore their master to pieces."

Artemis turned to stir the burning embers with a stick. In the darkness it seemed to the others that she became for a moment an old, woman, stooped and bent, her face lined.

Above: DIANA'S HUNT, *Domenico Zampieri (1581–1641).*

She then seemed like her youthful self, then the mature mother, in quick succession. Artemis indeed held within her the three faces of the goddess of ancient times, the Virgin, the Mother and the Crone.

"Thus do I value my privacy and my sacred virginity," she said, emphasizing each word. "And so must you."

The older nymphs and the young girls were silent for a time in the cool, dark night. As they settled down to sleep on their beds of leaves, they whispered, "We belong to ourselves alone. We are wild and free."

Athena

❖

Greece

Agoddess of supreme intelligence, Athena was one of the most complex and revered goddesses of the ancient Greeks. She was worshiped as the protectress of Athens, the Virgin Queen, whose temple the Parthenon stands above the city. Known to the Romans as Minerva, Athena was patroness of the arts and artisans, smiths and potters, spinners and weavers.

She was always a civilizing influence, who stood against the more unruly of the gods such as Hermes (Mercury) and Poseidon (Neptune).

Descended from the Titans, the oldest of the Greek gods, who ruled before the Olympians were established as the new gods by Zeus (Jupiter), Athena has ancient wisdom in her heritage. Attended by an owl, the wisest bird, and snakes, which connected her to the earth wisdom, Athena blended the old goddess and the new intelligence in Greek mythology. She was the mistress of weaving and her

Left: Marble statue detail of Athena from Varvakeion, with sacred horse helmet, c.400 BC.

ability to interweave the threads of life is a quality which always belongs to the greatest of goddesses.

Athena, though widely worshiped in Greece, was probably Cretan in origin (around 2000–1400 BC), as images of a shielded goddess accompanied Minoan and Mycenaean princes in the pose of wise teacher. The myth of her birth is from Hesiod (c.700 BC)

MYTHS OF ATHENA

Long ago, great and thunderous Zeus married the Titan sea goddess Metis who was pregnant with his child. Metis was as old as time itself and was known to be the wisest of all the gods, for she was revered for her gift of foresight and prophecy. It had once been predicted to Zeus that Metis would bear him first a daughter who would be the wisest of all the goddesses; however, should she then bear a son, he would become the Lord of all the Heavens. Supreme Zeus, intent on maintaining his exalted position as the ruler of the gods, decided to destroy Metis so that no such son could overthrow him.

It came to Zeus that by swallowing wise Metis he would increase his own wisdom, thus adding to his attributes that of prophecy as well as the ability of Metis to change shape. It was by entering into a wager with Metis that she

Right: Bronze figurine of Minerva by Girolamo Campagna (1549–c.1625).

41

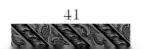

could not change into something as small as a fly that he was able to swallow her and the unborn baby whole.

Some time later, as he was walking by a lake in Crete, Zeus was suddenly beset by a blinding headache. He put his hands up to his head and cried out in pain. The silversmith of Mount Olympus, Hephaestus, came running to the cry, for Zeus, while known for his rages, was rarely known to express physical pain. Zeus tore at his hair and mopped the sweat from his eyes. He commanded Hephaestus to fashion him an axe with which to cleave open his forehead. Zeus felt a presence behind his eyes that had to come out, or he would surely die from the pain of it.

With godly speed Hephaestus worked, quickly and silently. In a short time he passed to his father a double-edged Cretan axe. Without any ado, Zeus raised it to his head and with a mighty blow, split his own head apart, roaring like a wild bull.

From the gaping wound sprang the goddess Athena, fully grown and beautiful. She stood before her father in shining golden armor, a sword in her right hand, her brilliant eyes flashing. She was so glorious, so powerful, that the whole earth quaked before her. For a time the sun ceased to shine, and the only light in the world radiated from the goddess Athena, as splendid as a star.

Left: Marble statue of Athena from west pediment of Temple of Aegina, Greece, 490 BC.

42

Even Zeus was momentarily silenced as he stared at her. Her grey eyes coolly met and held his gaze. So this was her fate, she thought, to have no mother and to be born from the head of this great and powerful god.

Zeus liked his daughter. He was proud of her bearing and the intelligence in her round grey eyes. He even liked the owl which swooped around her head and the snakes which hissed at her feet, for they invested her with the qualities of the goddesses of old. But Zeus did not appreciate how the whole world dimmed beside her glory.

"If you would be my daughter, and stand beside me on Mount Olympus as my friend and wise counsellor, dim your radiance, cool your fire," Zeus said to the shimmering maid. "There is room for only one brilliance here."

So Athena, wise from the mother she never knew, dimmed her glory and deferred to her father. She removed her gleaming armor and put aside her sword. The birds resumed their song, but not quite so sweetly as before. The sun shone once more upon the heavens and the earth, yet even some of its fire seemed to have been quenched as well.

Zeus placed his own sword in his daughter's hand and the cloak with his godly emblem across her shoulders, yet they did not suit her as well as had her own glorious armor. He welcomed Athena as his favorite child, his confidant and closest friend. Yet at

Right: Athena with serpent shield, which shows her connection to much earlier goddesses. Reproduction of the parthenon Athena by Phidias, original erected 447 BC.

43

times she wondered about her mother, who had known the wisdom of all the seas, had understood the tides which underlie the shifts and changes of countries and leaders, mythologies and gods. Athena kept all these things in her heart and outwardly developed her great intelligence and her love of beauty and the arts. She taught the crafts of spinning and weaving, of silver and gold, of creating musical instruments, of bridling the horse and of yoking the ox. From her earliest memories of the seas, she created the ship. The waters of knowledge lapped against her mind as Athena continued to take her place amid gods and men. "Athena, use your wisdom," whispered an ancient voice within her. "Help all who truly strive." So Athena befriended brave men and artists, guided and encouraged them.

Poseidon, lord of the seas, battled with her for supremacy, for memories ran deep inside him of the times long ago when goddesses had also held power in the great and mysterious deeps. At one time Poseidon disputed with Athena over which of them should give their name to the greatest city of Greece. The gods stated that whichever of the two could present the most useful gift to the inhabitants of the earth would win the contest. Poseidon offered first the great and changeable sea.

Athena observed quietly, "The sea will not be of much use to the people of my city, though in time they will rule the seas as my ancestors, the Cretans, once did."

Poseidon roared, "No people will ever rule me for I am mightier than all! Take this gift as well then!" and he struck the earth with his trident. Galloping from the opened earth came a magnificent horse, wild and beautiful to see.

Athena looked on with a calm, untroubled expression, listening within to her guiding voice. Standing tall, she struck the earth with her sword, sending her owl screeching high above her head. Where she had touched, the earth broke apart

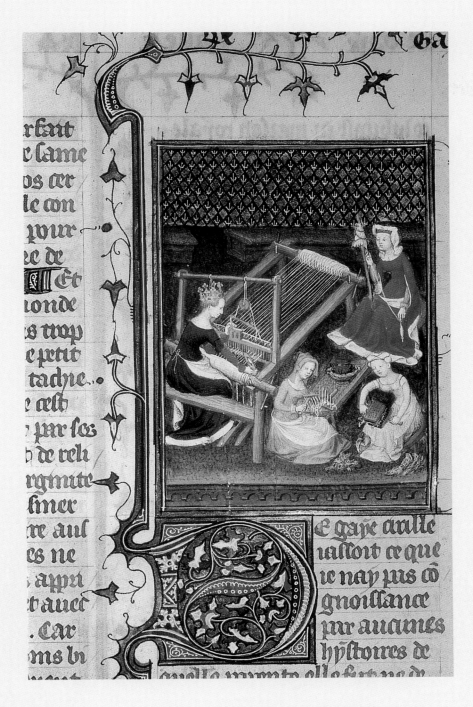

Above: Athena was the Greek goddess of spinning and weaving.
Detail from De Claris Mulieribus, *Giovanni Boccaccio (1313–1375)*

and green shoots appeared. As the gods looked on, a beautiful tree with grey-green leaves began to grow until all stood in its shade. Its trunk was strong and gnarled and from its branches hung fruit, growing from green to ripe purple-black. Athena's sacred snakes hissed joyfully and twirled around the strong trunk; her owl perched in the full branches and blinked.

"This is the First Olive Tree," Athena said. "It may be harvested for its fruit and for its oil. My people may use it for cooking, for preserving, for burning in their lamps at night, and for anointing their bodies that they may feel supple and smooth."

She raised her hand in tribute to the tree, sprung from the scant earth of Attica, saying, "The olive tree shall henceforward be sacred to me."

The gods unanimously voted that Athena's gift was the more useful and its branch once offered became the symbol of peace-making. The horse on the other hand, while useful, was more associated with war. Poseidon retreated to the sea, lashing the waves into an enraged frenzy, for he knew when he was beaten. Thus, the gods long ago decided that a peaceful gift would outweigh one which encouraged war and the name of Athens was chosen. On the Acropolis a great temple was built in honor of the goddess of the city, Athena, which even today stands sentinel, overlooking all.

Left: Detail of ATHENA WITH THE MUSES, *Jacques de Stella (1596–1657).*

Circe

Greece

A daughter of the sun god Helios, Circe was much celebrated as a witch, for she had great knowledge of magic and herbs for healing and craft. Circe was able to turn humans into pigs and other animals through her understanding of magic. A goddess of death and the underworld, Circe lived on the funerary island of Aeaea off the coast of Italy. Aeaea means "wailing", and Circe's sacred bird was the falcon, the death-bird. Circe's name was related to the circle, and she became associated with the turning of the cosmic spinning wheel which spun the fates of men.

This story of Circe and Odysseus (Ulysses) is told by Homer (c.900 BC) in the Iliad, and by Hesiod. (c.700 BC)

MYTH OF CIRCE AND ODYSSEUS

While sailing home to Greece from fighting the Trojan War, Odysseus and his crew were flung far off course. They came instead to the island of Aeaea, where the daughter of the sun lived, the golden-haired enchantress, Circe. When they had rested on the shore and were refreshed, Odysseus decided to explore the island for any sign of life. He found a high hill and scanned the surrounding land. At first no habitation was visible, but then he spied a lovely palace set in a pretty glade of trees and flowers. After discussion with the crew, it was decided that an advance party should go ahead to investigate. They drew lots and Odysseus and his group were selected to

wait on the shore while the other group ventured out to make contact with the local inhabitants.

When the small band approached the grove where the palace stood, they found themselves surrounded by fearsome beasts, wolves and lions. Terrified, the men reached for their weapons, prepared to fight. The creatures ignored the weapons and rolled over on their backs, attempting to lick the hands and faces of the men as if in greeting a master after a long day's absence. Although this band could not understand the reaction of the

Above: Circe depicted with her magic wand. THE GODDESS CIRCE, *Giovanni Battista Luteri Dossi (1489–1490).*

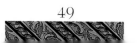

Above: Circe, *Giovanni Castiglione (1610–1670).*

beasts, they somehow felt encouraged to go on. What they did not know was that these creatures with the outward appearance of beasts were really men with men's consciousness — they had been enchanted by the powerful magic of the goddess Circe.

As the band of men approached the entrance to the palace, they could hear the sounds of music and laughter, the odor of delicious food and the sweet perfume of women. Their leader Eurylochus hid in the bushes and waited. Circe graciously welcomed the men inside, bade them sit down, eat, drink and listen to the music. Servants placed before the men food such as they had never seen, and strong, exotic wine. The men fell upon the food, vowing they had never tasted such dishes, such subtlety of flavors, such mixtures; they had been at sea a long time and had often eaten poor and tasteless fare. While they ate, Circe worked before a large loom, weaving a cloth of miraculous design and intricate pattern. As she worked, she sang a mysterious melody. The men became drowsy and soon they were half asleep.

Eurylochus, watching, started in horror as the goddess Circe approached the men and flicked each one with the end of a wand of delicately wrought gold, all the time muttering words in a strange language. Before his eyes, one by one the men were turned into huge pigs, with curving tusks and flapping ears. Pigs which ran about in terror, grunting and squealing, nudging each other with desperation. Circe summoned her swineherds who drove the new herd screaming into sties at the back of the palace.

"Feed these fellows good pig food," Circe cried, laughing scornfully. "Kitchen scraps and acorns will do them nicely."

Eurylochus ran with the terrible news to Odysseus and the waiting band on the shore. Odysseus became grim. He clapped a strong hand on Eurylochus' shoulder. "Wait here, my friend. I shall go alone to see this Circe, and I will retrieve my men."

Eurylochus begged to accompany Odysseus, but in vain, and the wily leader set off to the palace of Circe alone. On the way he met a handsome young man who called to him. "Sir, I know you are Odysseus, famous for your bravery and exploits, returning home from Troy."

Odysseus nodded curtly and the youth went on to say that he was Hermes (Mercury), messenger of the gods, come to offer service to Odysseus.

"Circe is a powerful enchantress," Hermes said. "In order to protect yourself from her magic you must carry some of this white flower which grows roundabout. It is called 'moly' and it will protect you from her enchantment. When she attempts to charm you, you must threaten her with your sword. Then she will agree to release your men. If she lures you to her bed, you must exact a promise from her that she will not rob you of your manhood. My advice to you, though, is to set sail immediately and put many miles between yourself and this island."

Odysseus thanked Hermes, but said firmly, "I am responsible for my men. I will restore them to their homes."

Hermes smiled, wished Odysseus good fortune, set off on his winged feet and Odysseus proceeded to the palace to meet the beautiful and dangerous Circe.

Bright and glorious like the sun, Circe of the Braided Hair greeted Odysseus with the same deceptive courtesy as she had his men. He was served the same food and wine, and as before, Circe entertained him, singing before her loom, dark thoughts behind her veiled eyes. When Odysseus pretended to fall asleep she touched him with that same magical wand, uttering those fearful words taught to her long ago. But the man sat unchanged before her, glad of the moly inside his shirt pressed against his heart.

"Go, join your friends in the piggery, sailor," she jeered, but found herself seized by a rough hand and felt the sharp edge of steel on her smooth throat.

"No, lady," Odysseus said, his tone as cruel as hers. "Release my men to their human form, or you die."

Circe, had smelt the moly upon Odysseus and knew the gods were with him. She fell before him, enjoying the game,

Above: CIRCE OFFERING THE CUP TO ULYSSES (ODYSSEUS),
John William Waterhouse (1849–1917).

looking up into his face. "Hermes told me to expect you, Odysseus the brave. Look to the doorway, your men are free already."

A little taken aback, Odysseus watched his men enter, looking taller, more manly, and more handsome than before. Circe glided towards them holding out her hands. "Come, join your master. Odysseus, you and your men may stay as my guests in my palace as long as you desire."

Odysseus frowned as he watched the men being entertained by the beautiful maidens who attended Circe and lived in the palace. Though he was mad with desire for her, Odysseus returned to collect the rest of his crew who were waiting anxiously on the shore. Unanimously they decided to enjoy the hospitality of Circe, for all were battle and travel-weary. As for Odysseus, the scent of that clever enchantress was in his clothing, in his mind and raging through his body.

Smiling to herself, Circe took the blood-red yarn and wove it deftly around the yellow, the color of her hair. One knot and a smaller thread of pale gossamer silk were stitched into the two. There, it was done, their fates were now woven.

Circe faced Odysseus eye to eye, for she was as tall as he and as powerful as he could imagine, and she smiled. "Odysseus, come to my bed, that we may sweetly meet and learn to trust one another." She took his arm and slowly walked towards her chambers. Before the doorway to the bedroom Odysseus stopped, his hand on the hilt of his dagger.

"You must promise never to rob me of my manhood, for I will kill you first!" She laughed into his face. "Hermes has taught you well Odysseus. Come, you will be safe with me, I promise."

That night a boy child was conceived, just as prophesied to Circe by the messenger Hermes. As Odysseus lay sleeping, the lines of exhaustion fading from his face, Circe hummed in her strange, haunting voice. She knew that they would remain

together for thirteen cycles of the moon, merging their magic and cunning, strength and power. It was long ago that the Great Goddess had set this tradition by choosing as her consort a man of unusual beauty or ability, and had kept him by her for one year, that all the seasons should rotate in their love.

"I will help you, father of my son," she whispered. "You have far to travel in distance and in story. You will carry my name into the future where such things are no longer believed. I will continue to instruct you, for you have much to learn, and I am lonely for one such as you." Affection stirred in the Circe's heart for the tough, loyal man before her, and she lay her head on the pillow and slept soundly in his arms.

Above: THE SORCERESS CIRCE WITH THE COMPANIONS OF ODYSSEUS THAT HAVE BEEN TRANSFORMED INTO ANIMALS, *fresco, Alessandro Allori, (1535–1607).*

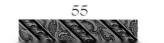

Daphne

Greece

Daphne was a priestess of Gaia (known as Tellus to the Roman world), the Mother Earth. While not a goddess, Daphne came to be loved by the god Apollo and was thus immortalized. Described as a beautiful priestess of extraordinary oracular power, Daphne led secret women's rituals in celebration of the power of Mother Earth. Shrines and oracles are dedicated to her in various places in Asia Minor but her main temple was at Tempe near Mount Olympus. The story of Daphne's flight from Apollo became the inspiration of many paintings and poems. The laurel became Daphne's sacred tree and also the tree of poetic inspiration. From ancient times, laurel wreaths were placed upon the heads of the best poets. To this day chosen poets are called poet "laureate" or laurel-crowned.

The following story was first recorded by the Roman poet, Ovid, born 43 BC.

MYTH OF DAPHNE

Deep in the woods, by the vale of Tempe, near the great Mount Olympus, priestesses had gathered to celebrate Gaia, the Mother Earth. Daphne, glorious in her sacred garment stood out among the other beautiful initiates. There was something marvelous in the tilt of her chin as she spoke the mysterious words, kept safe for so many years by the women who loved the earth. When Daphne spoke of autumn, the

Above: APOLLO AND DAPHNE, *Gerard Hoet (1648–1733).*

colors of falling leaves shimmered on her face; when she spoke of the waters, her whole body rippled and swayed. When she spoke of earth, the air seemed to still as though the gathered were suddenly in a great cavern of damp mosses. A hush descended when Daphne uttered the ancient name of the earth goddess, from which her own name derived, "Daphoene..."

The mortal Leucippus, in his wish to draw closer to Daphne, had decided to infiltrate the secret ceremonies by dressing as a woman. Demurely robed, he stood at the back of the gathered women, transfixed by Daphne's face. Unbeknown to Leucippus, he was not the only admirer of Daphne; the sun god Apollo was also observing the scene from above. Apollo, well known for his ruthlessness, decided to put a horrible end to his rival by alerting his twin, the fierce

Above: Daphne transforming into the laurel tree. APOLLO AND DAPHNE, *Paolo Caliari Veronese (1528–1588).*

huntress Artemis. With her attendants, Artemis swiftly surrounded Leucippus and tore him apart as punishment for his sacrilege.

Apollo, for his own lustful reasons, suggested that in future the priestesses should perform their ceremonies naked, so that such a deception should never happen again. Grateful to cunning Apollo for his help, the priestesses agreed to his suggestion, and at the next ceremony they appeared nude. Apollo, watching lasciviously, became so enamored with Daphne he decided to seize her without further ado. However

the nymph was as chaste as she was beautiful and, hearing news of the sun god's desire, became so distressed she immediately made plans to escape Tempe.

Apollo who sees all, flew straight to her side and pleaded with her, "Beautiful Daphne, come with me to Mount Olympus and be mine."

"I thank you sire, but I belong to Gaia alone," she said, averting her eyes. "I can love no other, neither god nor man."

Apollo grew angry. He bore down upon her with menace in his step. Much afraid, Daphne prayed that swift wings would adhere to her ankles and began to flee. Apollo pursued her with all the determination of his nature. Though a great god, he had been unlucky in love thus far. He felt assured that Daphne, once under his spell, would heal his wounded heart and bring him bliss. Apollo was determined. "I must have her," he said, as he followed her fleeing figure, "whether she is willing or not."

Daphne felt the strength ebb from her body. Her fear had lent her speed, but to outrun Apollo was impossible. His step sounded like thunder behind her, before her and beside her. Afraid, with nowhere to turn, Daphne felt his breath harsh upon her ear.

"Stop, little one. You will never escape me. Surrender to the god," he said.

Daphne screamed to the Earth Mother to whom she had devoted her life. "Mother! Save me!" She looked around wildly. Her gaze fell upon a laurel tree standing nearby. "Change me into that laurel, that I may escape!"

Gaia heard her plea. She reached up quickly, encircling Daphne, and absorbed her into the waiting branches of the laurel. "Rest here, beloved child." The voice of Gaia rustled through the leaves. "You are safe. No harm can come to you. You have become everlasting, the essence of the laurel tree."

Apollo cried out in fury, impotent before the power of the Mother Earth. He bellowed in rage. Then, haltingly at first, his tears began to flow, and with his head pressed upon the trunk of the tree which held Daphne, Apollo cried out his tears of pain. Eventually, all passion spent, he gently picked a branch of the laurel which he fashioned into a circlet.

Placing the wreath upon his head, the great shining Apollo knelt upon his godly knee before the tree. "Daphne," he said softly, a more mature tone entering his voice. "I shall in future wear this wreath in honor of you. My brutish behavior has harmed you, and I have lost you. Oh Daphne, you shall ever be my inspiration."

The laurel only sighed, nestling its roots more firmly into the earth. Daphne, whose name was now Laurel, felt safe and at peace. She knew that Apollo had undergone a change as surely as she, and would now become more reasoned, more moderate in his behavior. He would henceforward encourage the arts, especially poetry. For her part she would gladly give her branches as wreaths for the most eloquent poets of the world.

Right: THE METAMORPHOSIS OF DAPHNE INTO A LAUREL TREE BY APOLLO, *Charles Sims (1873–1928).*

Demeter

⬡

Greece

Demeter was the goddess of the fertile earth, the grain, and of all the fruits of the earth. The name Demeter is probably derived from the Cretan word for grain, *dyai*. Gaia, not Demeter, was the goddess of the whole earth, while Demeter was the goddess of the cultivated earth with all its fruits. She was also goddess of the dead, who were called Demeter's People, for they returned to fertilize the earth. To symbolize this, corn was scattered on the graves of the newly dead. The myth of Demeter is inseparable from that of her daughter, Persephone, so they may be seen as aspects of each other. One is the maiden and one the mature woman. The third face of the triple goddess is shown by the appearance of Hecate as the older woman, or crone. In Roman mythology Demeter and Persephone were called Ceres and Proserpina.

The following myth is an adaptation of the classical Greek myth, the Rape of Persephone, which explains the seasons. Earlier myths suggest that Persephone entered the underworld of her own free will, like Inanna of Sumaria, and Ishtar of Babylon.

Left: Marble statue of Demeter, Greece, c.330 BC.

62

MYTH OF DEMETER AND PERSEPHONE

Long ago there was no winter on the earth. The fruits of trees, vines and soil grew abundantly, withered and died, then began to grow again in slow and natural cycles. The only rhythm which could be clearly observed was that of the ever-changing moon. Humans gathered the edible fruits and berries and planted vegetables. They learned what was good to eat, and what was not. In that time it is said that Zeus (Jupiter) seduced Demeter, goddess of the fertile earth, and that she bore a daughter, Persephone. The mother and her child rejoiced in each other's company. They walked, arms entwined as Demeter maintained the fertility of the vegetable crops, the fruiting of the trees and the care of the earth. One day Persephone wandered off with some friends on the plains of Nysa. She was so struck by the beauty of a rare flower called narcissus, that she bent down to pick it. At that moment, the earth gaped wide. Hades, god of the underworld, emerged from the depths in a golden chariot pulled by rearing black horses. Like swift death he seized her and carried her screaming in terror to Erebus, the place of darkness.

Demeter, realizing harm had come to her beloved daughter, searched vainly for nine long days and nine long nights. She wandered far and near, asking all she met for news of Persephone. Only Hecate, crone goddess of the crossroads, spoke to her.

"I did hear Persephone cry out," she said sadly, "And I heard the abductor speak, but it was very faint, very far off."

Demeter's fine clothing was in rags. Her glorious hair hung in dirty tatters. She was insane with grief. Where her feet touched, the earth lay parched and desolate. Crops withered in the ground as the goddess passed by. Women and

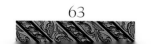

she-animals miscarried, and if they were nursing infants the milk dried up in their breasts.

"Woe is come upon the land," cried the people, throwing up their hands. "Our grounds are cursed. Our trees are dying. Our wells have dried up. We shall all die!"

In great anguish Demeter turned to Helios (Sol), the sun god who sees all on his journey across the heavens daily. "Have you seen my daughter? My lovely maid? What god or human has done this thing?"

Helios responded gravely, "You need blame none other than Zeus, the father of your daughter, for he has given Persephone to Hades, for a wife."

Demeter great dark eyes flashed in anger. "Then, by my life, nothing shall remain upon this earth Zeus holds so dear. For humans cannot live without my blessing, and that blessing I withdraw."

So saying, she turned and resumed her wanderings upon the wasted lands, lighting her way by night with huge torches which scorched the trees and grasses, until no bird song could be heard, no buzzing of bees, no scurrying of ants underfoot.

"The earth is dying," sobbed one person to the other. "We can but watch and pray. Where is the goddess Demeter, goddess of the green earth? Where can she be?"

Demeter, heedless of their supplications, walked on. Throughout all those long days and nights she took no nourishment, took no water.

On the ninth day Demeter came to a well near Eleusis, not far from Athens, and sat down, her divinity hidden by rags, grief eating her from within. Baubo, a woman of good humor even in those times of darkness, stood by the well trying to draw water, though it was very low.

"Hey mistress, you don't look well," she laughed. "Let me draw some water for you as well as me!"

It was a joke, for there was so little for anyone. Demeter remained locked within her grief, not responding to Baubo.

Above: Demeter (Ceres), the goddess of fertility and abundance.
CERES, *Baldassare Peruzzi (1481–1536).*

"Ho Mistress, things can't be that bad!" Baubo called, and began to pull faces and make tricks. Still to no avail. Finally Baubo threw her apron and skirts above her head and ran about jumping and kicking.

Distracted from her grieving, Demeter began to smile. Soon she was laughing, and the grass grew green all around her.

Above: Demeter (Ceres) as the abundant earth goddess.
STATUE OF CERES, *Peter Paul Rubens (1577–1640)*

Water gurgled in the well and rose magically to the top, until it overflowed. Baubo settled her skirts around her naked body and gave a wide smile.

"That's better," she said, looking around for the old ragged woman. But there before her was the glorious goddess of the fertile earth herself, garlanded in greens and golds and fruits of all kinds. Baubo ran to the village. There she told the story and the people came to the well. This well was foreverafter sacred to Demeter, as was the whole of Eleusis. It was here at Eleusis for many thousands of years that the mystery of Demeter and Persephone and their reunion would be celebrated.

Meanwhile, Zeus viewed with anger and alarm the disastrous famine spreading over the earth. If all humans were annihilated there would be no more sport with beautiful human maidens, no sacrifices nor proper worship of the gods. Zeus stormed about the sky, punching his huge fist into his hand until thunder roared and lightening split the sky from Athens to Anatolia. Zeus sent a succession of envoys to speak with Demeter, all to no avail. Finally he sent for his messenger Hermes, and ordered him to go to Hades with instructions that Persephone must be returned to her mother immediately, or all life on earth would cease. Hades seemed to agree to this order, but urged Persephone to eat a pomegranate seed before he lifted her into the golden chariot which was to carry her back to the earth. Persephone was glad to eat the seed, she was so excited at the thought of seeing her mother again.

The ground opened up and Persephone was placed once more on the earth. Where she trod the grass leapt to her footstep, vivid and green. Birds began to sing as blossoms burst into bloom on every tree. As Demeter ran to gather Persephone into her arms, rivers gurgled with joy, and vegetables unfurled

from their places in the stony earth and pushed through green shoots of exultant life. The people wept for joy.

"We are saved," cried the people all over the land. "Our world will survive."

But Demeter questioned Persephone closely about her experience, and asked if her daughter had eaten any food in the kingdom of the dead. When she heard of the pomegranate seed, Demeter bowed her head to hide her tears, but Persephone asked, "Mother! What does this mean?"

"My child, when you have eaten the food of death, it ties you to the underworld." Demeter folded her lips with resignation, for such laws went back before time itself and could not be questioned. She resolved to negotiate with the gods, now that they had witnessed the effect of separation from her daughter. Finally a compromise was struck with Hades that for nine months of the year Demeter and Persephone would live in joy together in the world of the living. During the other three months, Persephone would return to the underworld as queen, as the bride of Hades. But in those three months, Demeter would grieve for her daughter, relinquishing her responsibility for the earth. Nothing would grow and the season of winter would be upon the land. Then, in a time which would be known as Spring, Persephone would return and the world would bloom anew. Demeter however was so grateful to be reunited with Persephone that she gave humans the gift of grain, which had previously been unknown on the earth. "Take this grain", said the great corn goddess to the first farmer of Eleusis, "that you may store food for the three months when I do not tend the earth and must grieve my daughter."

Demeter taught the people how to grow the crops and store the seed, so they would not hunger in the cold months. In this way the ebb and flow of the seasons was settled.

Above: Demeter handing the gift of grain to an Eleusinian youth, while Persphone looks on. Stone relief, 440–430 BC.

Flora

Rome

Flora, whose name means "The Flourishing One", was the ancient Italian goddess of the springtime. Flora was the goddess of the budding and burgeoning earth after the long winter cold, and was sometimes known as Primavera, which means Spring.

Feronia, another Roman goddess, shared many of the functions of Flora. However, Feronia was a goddess of the underworld, the symbolic place from which Flora emerged bringing the springtime. As goddess of vines, fruit trees, blossoms, flowers and cereals, Flora was much welcomed into the lives of the ancients on her festivals, the Floralia, and the Rose festival celebrated on the twenty third of May. Flora's festival is similar to the European May Day festival, when Maj or Mai, the Virgin, emerges from the earth. May was the traditional month of "wearing the green", the color of the earth in its spring garment. May Day is still celebrated today in several countries.

The Floralia lasted from the twenty eighth of April until the third of May, amid much feasting, drinking, flinging off of clothing and lovemaking. Speaking disapprovingly of the Floralia, a contemporary writer Lactantius commented that Flora was a "Lady of Pleasure". However, her festival was much loved and central to the early Roman religion which was still linked to the seasons. It was even said that Flora was the secret soul name of great Rome itself.

Her worship was firmly stamped out by St Augustine and other early fathers of the Christian church, who said she incited nudity and licentious behavior among the people.

Above: The goddess Flora. Roman fresco from Stabia near Naples, Italy.

MYTH OF FLORA

As the sun of early springtime warmed the earth, as though overnight, sweet, green shoots appeared on every patch of ground. In those days the spring was loved for its greening of the earth, but as yet no flowers graced the world. People flung open the doors of their dwellings and breathed the mild, fresh air. Animals, freed at last from their winter byres, sniffed and nuzzled the tender shoots and grasses.

One particular spring morning, so long ago it cannot be remembered except by poets and minstrels, a goddess stirred and awoke deep within the earth. Spreading wide her arms and stretching, she murmured, "I am called." Even in the darkness there was a glow about her, a radiance which lit the darkness, and where her hand speared upwards like a green shoot, the earth parted to her touch.

Soon the goddess found herself lying curled on the fresh grasses in a shady glade by a cool stream. She stepped lightly to the running water and refreshed herself, drinking deeply and splashing her face and neck. When the water had settled, she saw her own beauty reflected as glorious as the sun on fields of grain. Touching her hair, she frowned. Something was missing, but what?

Just then, Zephyrus (Favonius), the west wind, began to blow softly around her. Here was perfection to his eye. He fluttered gently about her hair and tugged at the hem of her gown. Then, gaining in confidence as she did not rebuff him, he began to swirl around her body, whispering, "Who are you? How came you here?"

Regarding his moving form with eyes as deep as the place from where she had come, she responded slowly, as if

Left: Flora, the goddess of Spring. Detail from LA PRIMAVERA, *Sandro Filipepi Botticelli (1445–1510).*

remembering. "I am Flora, goddess of the spring. I have come to be your bride."

"Welcome, beloved," he sighed, wrapping his warm arms around her. "I have waited for you so long."

Flora felt love quicken in her heart; her body ached to be held tightly and never to be let go, and her hands began to burn with a strange sensation.

"Come, my love," the wind whispered. "Let me show you the world."

As their lips met, the first rose bloomed. As their hands touched, all the trees on the earth burst into bud and blossomed. Birds sang a new song, bees buzzed with sheer delight, and the world rejoiced as nectar came into being, as well as honey and all the delights of perfume.

Above: FLORA'S TRIUMPH, *Nicolas Poussin (1594–1665).*

Flora reached down and picked the first flowers, and Zephyrus twisted them into her curling hair. They both laughed with happiness.

"This is what was missing," Flora said. "I shall wear flowers ever after in my hair, in honor of this day of flowers and our love which has brought them forth.

Flora was lifted in the arms of Zephyrus and as they flew to the four corners of the world, Flora's tingling fingers dropped the essences of flowers onto the earth. Zephyrus nuzzled the neck of his bride and a myriad of petals fell to earth like rain, attaching to plants and blooming anew, or settling in cracks and putting up buds. Where there was a place for a flower, one grew, each perfect for its surroundings. Great, bright hibiscus, sweet jasmine and starry frangipani fell to the warm zones; to the cooler climates, the fragrant rose, the shy lily of the valley, the pinks, the bluebells, the wild red-black peonies.

In mountainous snowy regions fell the pasque flower, the bristling alpine eryngium and the essence of edelweiss. To the desert, Flora dropped her dewy substance so that the cactus could now flower in spiky glory, and the clinging, spidery rock flowers could bloom when the rains came.

The world was alight with flowers, radiant with blooms, drowning in the new scent of being. Everywhere lovers reached out for each other, yearning to touch, that day the flowers were born.

Hathor

❖

Egypt

It is difficult to imagine a goddess as diverse as Hathor who was one of the prime divinities of Western civilization. She was a manifestation of the Great Mother Goddess who was worshiped in prehistoric times in the red earth of the north of Egypt. Worshiped for more than 3000 years in Ancient Egypt, and as far afield as Somalia, the Sinai peninsular and Phoenicia, Hathor was believed to nourish all the living with her milk, and was the protectress of women and female animals. Over such a long period of time, many varied legends and stories grew up surrounding Hathor and her roles, though in general she symbolized laws that never change. In Egyptian art, one of Hathor's most familiar forms was the winged cow of creation giving birth to the universe. Thus she was seen as an eternal, life-supporting principle (see Ancient Mother Goddess page 10). The Great Goddess when she appears is always complex, and embodies many conflicting aspects of the feminine. She ruled over life, death and the afterlife.

Left: Detail of statue of Hathor at Luxor, showing her cow horns holding the sun.

Like Demeter who came after her in Greece, Hathor had sovereignty over the bodies of the dead because she had given birth to them. Hathor embodied the triple goddess, queen of the underworld as well as the Earth and Sky, in accordance with the three phases of the moon. In the Egyptian Book of the Dead, she is depicted as the "good cow", half emerging from the Libyan Mountain, welcoming the dead to that westernmost point of Ancient Egypt. (see pic. p. 79) It was believed that those who beseeched her in the correct manner would be safely carried to the afterlife on her back.

In early times the Goddess often took her son as her husband; this practice is known as uniting with the "son-lover". The male in this myth was seen as representing a principle which would be born, then die and be reborn again as we see in the following myth of Hathor and Horus which dates from around 3000 BC.

MYTH OF HATHOR

From the swirling chaos of the primeval waters emerged a hill upon which stood a magnificent wild ox cow. Stretching, the cow goddess expressed some of her many forms. She manifested as a great and beautiful woman, stretching across the sky, touching the earth with only the tips of her fingers and toes. The people called her Nut. Now she was a huge lioness with eyes of fire. The people called her Sekhmet. Then she became the beautiful sycamore tree shading the edge of the desert. The people revered her as the living presence of the goddess and called her "Lady of the Sycamore". Using her sacred wood they crafted the coffins of kings, that the dead might be carried in her womb to the afterlife. Finally, as Great Hathor, Wild Ox, Mother of All, she stretched out her legs and placed them carefully upon the four corners of the earth.

Above: Painted limestone relief of the goddess Hathor placing the magic collar on Sethi 1, taken from the tomb of Sethi 1 in the Valley of the Kings, New Kingdom, 19th dynasty, c.1314–1200 BC.

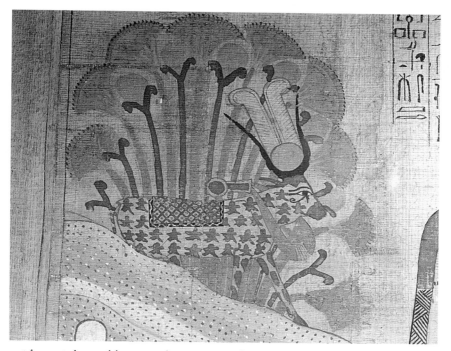

Above: The goddess Hathor, in cow shape, emerging from the western hill, from The Book of the Dead of Userhtemos, *19th dynasty, c.1295–1186 BC.*

"These will be the North, the South, the East and the West," she said, as the starry firmament twinkled on her belly.

The people bowed down before her greatness, saying, "We will seek the Cow Mother. Great is the Wild Ox of the marshes. She will nourish us on earth, then she will take us to the great After."

"I will be known as Hathor to my people," she said. "My name means 'House of Horus' so I shall bring forth a son, who will be as good and constant as he is beautiful. He shall be my companion, my husband, and my love." So saying, she gave birth to a son and called him Horus.

"Dear one, you shall be the golden falcon who will fly across the sky. In the morning you will bring the sun god from the east, and take him to the west in the evening. There I will greet you as my husband. In the night we will be together.

You will stay within my body, traveling. This will be your duty from now until I choose to end life on earth."

Horus listened gravely. He flexed his new glorious wings, strong and golden, and with joy prepared himself.

"I will undertake this journey forever," he promised. "I will journey over the rich and the poor. I will journey over the warring and the peaceful. I will give light to the rain storms and to the cloudless sky. Each night I shall return to my Beloved, and dwell within her. Thus I have been instructed by my Mother, my wife, who knows the destiny of all."

As he flew in the easterly direction, the fierce sun blazed on Egypt all day. Approaching the west, he pushed the setting sun before him into the mouth of Hathor, his mother and wife, while Egypt rested in the welcome cool. All night long he stayed in the house of his mother, traveling the vast distance inside her long, starry body. In the morning, Horus was born again pushing the sun before him, his mother's blood red at the dawn. So it happened for more years than can be counted.

As the cycles repeated, Hathor watched over her peoples. Joyful herself, she wanted sensuous delight to be celebrated upon the earth. She caused artists to imagine her in many beautiful, womanly forms, adorned with glorious jewels and garments. Her priestesses followed her example and dressed themselves in beauty, garlanded with flowers. Hathor inspired music to be born, to reflect upon and embellish the glory of life and love. Dancing and leaping the priestesses revered the goddess. Playing music and singing, they remembered her name. Her festivals became a time for rejoicing, merriment and for making love. The love of music she inspired in her people was so intense they built a great Temple of Hathor at the place called Denderah. Each of the columns was conceived as a part of the musical instrument Hathor loved best, the sistrum. To enter this temple was to worship within music, to

*Above: The Pharoah Amenophis II drinks from
the udder of the cow goddess, Hathor, wall painting from
a chapel built by Tuthmosis III, Weir el Bahri.*

become music itself. People made small sistrums, which were said to ward off evil spirits as well as to fill the heart with joy.

On New Year's Day at dawn, her priestesses wheeled an immense statue of Hathor to the east of the temple, so that she could receive the first rays of the born-again sun. It is said that the goddess spoke aloud to Horus, and these words were written in the great Pyramid Texts:

"Take my breast, that you may drink, so that you may live again."

Thus the people remembered Hathor's promise to nourish all her people, in life and in the hereafter. In joy and remembrance, the great festival began. The special, blood-red liquor brewed especially for the goddess in her form as Sekhmet, was consumed in plenty. Sounds of laughter, drinking vessels being filled to overflowing, the murmurs of lovers, and all kinds of revelry filled the air.

Isis

Egypt

I sis is the Greek name for the great Egyptian goddess Au Set, queen of heaven, earth and underworld. Isis in Greek means literally "Ancient Ancient". She was worshiped far beyond Egypt for more than 3000 years until the second century AD. At that time her cult and many of her images passed on to Mary. Like Mary, Isis appears as the Mother Goddess with her son Horus on her knee. At a certain time in pre-dynastic Egypt, Hathor and Isis, who both had a son Horus, were blended with Nut the sky goddess to become the one mother of all the pharaohs of Egypt.

The power and patience of love is the gift Isis brings from thousands of years ago.

Of the many myths about Isis, the most famous is the story of her love for Osiris. Inscribed in beautiful hieroglyphs, *The Great Hymn to Isis* is found in the Pyramid Texts, which come from 2491 BC–2181 BC. Later the myth was recorded by the Greek historian Plutarch (40–120 AD).

Left: Statue of Isis and the child Horus, bronze encrusted with gold, late period, 664–332 BC. Such images pre-dated the Christian Madonna with Child.

MYTH OF ISIS AND OSIRIS

Long ago in sacred time, the sky goddess Nut, and Geb, god of the earth, united to bring forth the gods and goddesses of Egypt. Many omens surrounded the birth of Osiris, who was the first born god. It is said that as darkness fell upon the earth at his birth a great voice cried, "Behold the Lord of all approaches the light." His brother Seth, furious not to be first born, slashed his way out of his mother's belly, using a huge knife. Some little time later, Isis was born quietly in the moist swamps of the Nile delta. Isis and Osiris loved each other even before birth, and following their promise in the womb, soon were married, a practice which was followed by the pharaohs who always wed their sisters.

Osiris became as great as his birth had prophesied. He became the civilizer of the seven black lands of Egypt, which, petal like, fanned out to form the Nile delta. Osiris traveled around teaching the laws which brought the tribes together in peace. Soon all were living untroubled up and down the Nile. With Isis as his wife, Osiris taught the people how to worship the gods, and gave them the magical secrets of seeds so that agriculture could develop in harmony with the yearly flooding of the Nile. Osiris instructed the people on the planting of fruits and vegetables, and soon the desert began to flower. Osiris and Isis were much loved, and the people revered Osiris as king. When Osiris traveled far and near, Isis ruled peacefully in his stead. Only one thing marred their happiness, they had no child.

Seth, from his place in the red lands, watched the successful reign of Osiris with smoldering rage. His jealousy reached such a peak that he decided to put a stop to Osiris once and for all. Spreading evil rumors about his brother, Seth gathered seventy two supporters around him and devised a plan that would not fail. He ordered a sarcophagus to be

made to the exact dimensions of Osiris. It was a fine cedarwood casket, inlaid with intricate gold and silver designs, with a perfectly fitting lid. Then Seth sent out invitations for all to attend a party, to be held in honor of Osiris. Such a party had never been seen before in Egypt. The musicians played through the night and the wine, food and exotic dancing were of such magnificence that Osiris felt overcome with pleasure.

"At last," Osiris thought, "the enmity between me and my brother is at an end. This is a very good day." With a glad heart he smiled benignly upon the assembled guests. At that very moment, Seth ordered the magnificent casket to be brought in and invited all to enter and admire it.

Osiris ran his fingers over the fine grain of the wood, wondered at the craftsmanship of the gold and silver inlay, and closing his eyes, relaxed back into it, marveling at the exact fit. Immediately Seth called upon his seventy two helpers who quickly nailed fast the sarcophagus, and filled every opening with molten lead. They then flung it into the Nile to finish their evil task. Thus entombed, Osiris floated towards the sea.

Isis tore her queenly clothes, cut off her beautiful hair and wandered up and down the kingdoms of the Nile crying, "Have you seen Osiris? Have you seen your king? Oh where is my dear husband?"

No one had seen the sarcophagus or its direction, and Isis was very tired from the long search. At last some children playing by the Nile said they had seen something strange floating towards the great green sea. Isis thanked them and blessed them saying, "All children will henceforward be as observant as you. Some will even be prophetic and speak of things to come." The children lowered their eyes, averting them from the strange lady who had suddenly transformed into a being of radiant light.

Above: Tomb painting of the departed before
Osiris, Isis and Thoth, c. 2850 BC.

Meanwhile Osiris had come to rest, still enclosed in his casket, on the shores of Byblos in Phoenicia, near a tamarisk tree. The godliness of the sarcophagus and its contents communicated itself to the tree and slowly the branches reached down and encircled it. Soon the tree had absorbed the sarcophagus into its trunk, and from that moment began to emit a glorious scent. Fame of the scented tree spread to the king and queen of Byblos who ordered that the tree be felled so that it could become the central pillar of their palace.

Following the godly scent of Osiris, Isis traveled to the coast of Phoenicia, veiled and in mourning, with her divinity

Above: Trinity of Osorkon II depicting Osiris flanked by Isis and Horus, gold and lapis lazuli, 22nd dynasty, 874–850 BC.

hidden by rags. At last she came to the palace. There Isis herself emitted such a fragrance that the queen asked the strange yet marvelous woman to stay and nurse the newborn baby prince, for it was well known that only the gods could smell so sweet. In the night Isis revealed her true nature to the queen by becoming a bird. A swallow, she swooped around the pillar concealing the body of her beloved, crying mournfully.

The queen bowed to Isis, allowing her to cut down the pillar and free the sarcophagus which still held Osiris. Isis returned the pillar to the queen and the watching king. Later the pillar was announced to be the most sacred object in their kingdom, for it had held the body of Osiris, the great god. Meanwhile, Isis set sail for Egypt with her dead Osiris, enclosed in his casket. She brought the boat to rest on a deserted bank in the marshes seeking to deceive Seth whom, she sensed, still followed. At last Isis opened the casket and fell upon the cold body of her sweet, dead love, her tears falling on his breast. She became a bird and flew above, fanning him with wings of gold. In her soft woman's body she lay with Osiris, heart to heart, and kissed his cool lips. Above him as an angel she fluttered life into his heart. Isis, goddess of the miraculous, drew forth his life. Osiris stirred, awoke, and held out his arms to his love. That long dark night, Isis and Osiris were lovers once more, and from their union a baby boy was conceived. Isis, smiling in the darkness, felt the baby Horus moving in her womb.

Seth, the wicked brother, crept through the marshes. When he saw the beautifully fashioned cedarwood sarcophagus he tore it apart. Hatred gave his hands strength; uttering terrible cries, Seth wrenched the body of Osiris into fourteen pieces and flung them far and wide.

"How great I am," Seth cried, mad with power and revenge. "It is not possible to destroy a god, but I have done it. Now may the crocodiles feast on him!" His fierce words echoed throughout the land, and all who heard shuddered and hid. Refusing to be daunted or dismayed by Seth's vile deed, Isis again went searching for her husband. As she recovered him, she slowly pieced Osiris together.

Isis and her helpers searched throughout the drought stricken lands of Egypt, until at last thirteen parts of Osiris were found. In each place where Isis found a piece of Osiris, she ordered a shrine built to his divinity. "Only when Osiris is made whole can the floods come," Isis told the silent villagers; and they went back to their homes and prayed for his restoration. Isis bound together his thirteen parts; then from her magic and the mud of the Nile, she created the phallus that had been lost. Finally when the fourteen parts were together in his likeness, Isis embalmed Osiris, showing her helpers what to do. Osiris thus became the first mummy of Egypt. Holding her hands high over his body, Isis spoke the words of life and death and delivered Osiris to the Great Beyond where he became Ruler of Eternity.

Later, Isis looked deeply into the eyes of her son Horus who would be the first pharaoh of Egypt.

Left: Roman sculpture of Isis bearing a close resemblance to Christian images of Mary. The cult and image of Isis passed on to the mother of Christ. c.250–300 AD.

Above: Stone relief of Isis from the tomb of Princess Yi, 18th Dynasty.

She placed him on her knee and held him close, feeling his small, warm body, trusting in her arms.

"I will always hold you in this way," she promised. "When you are king and your sons' sons are kings, I shall hold you all. I will be the throne of Egypt and you will sit always on my lap. My wings will enfold and protect you forever. You must fight the forces of darkness. One day good will triumph over evil, and Osiris your father will return."

Kali

India

In Indian mythology all the goddesses derive from one goddess source and are all aspects of each other. One of the most horrible and most venerated aspects of this force was Kali, which means Mother Time, Mighty Time or Endless Time. She is worshiped in India to this day, and her sacred city is Calcutta, Kali-Ghatt, which means, "steps of Kali". The goddess Kali is usually depicted as a fearsome four-armed figure, naked and with a garland of human heads around her neck. Her nakedness is said to indicate her freedom from this world's illusions.

The skulls which adorn her each represent one of the fifty letters of the Sanskrit alphabet. These magical rune-like letters symbolize the underlying principles and fundamental vibrations of the universe.

Right: Bronze statue of Kali,
late Chola period,
12th century.

Kali was thought to have brought the written word to the Indian peoples.

Although Kali may seem a terrifying figure, she is much loved by the Indian people. She is understood to be a complex goddess with many faces, both terrible and wonderful. Raksha-Kali, the Protectress, is worshiped in times of natural disaster, epidemic, famine, earthquake, drought and flood. In her somewhat gentler form, Shyama-Kali has a place of honor in Hindu households, where she answers prayers and grants boons. Contrary to her appearance Kali, when approached in the correct manner, dispels fear, cuts through pretence and illusion, and is the vehicle of bliss.

Kali's worship hails from c.400 AD though her myths are certainly much older.

Myths of Kali

BIRTH OF KALI

The goddess Kali first manifested herself when the demons seized divine power and threatened the kingdom of Shiva, the creator-destroyer, dancing god. At that time Shiva's wife Parvarti was battling the demons and assuming many terrifying shapes. In her battle form Parvarti was called Durga, and it was from the intense brow of Durga that Kali sprang, flashing her three eyes, her four arms waving weapons. Kali immediately set about dispensing the demons with great enjoyment. After the fighting was over, Parvarti tried to recall Kali, but once born, Kali would not be reabsorbed. She remained an aspect of Parvarti, but complete in herself, uncontrollable.

Kali, now unleashed, rolled her red tongue which dripped blood from her battle with the enemies of the gods. Her dark skin glowed, shining with the exertion, skulls rattled from her ear-rings, and severed hands hung from her girdle. Durga-Parvarti, surveyed Kali from astride her lion, saying, "From my brow you were born, yet you refuse to obey me."

Kali responded, "Durga, you must know me. I am Kali-Ma, great Mother Time. Neither god nor human can control me. When there was nothing, neither sun, nor moon, stars nor any world, I was there. Where there was darkness I held the seeds for the new universe. For I am the Formless One, Maha-Kali, the Great Power, Maha-Kali, the Absolute."

KALI AND RAKTAVIJA

Several famous myths tell of Kali's uncontrollable nature. Once she encountered and fought the greatest demon of all, Raktavija. Chief of a huge army of hideous demons, Raktavija sent them in legions to fight the goddess Kali until wave upon wave of demons lay slaughtered before her terrible rage. Fearing that Kali would destroy all of his soldiers, Raktavija decided to attack the goddess himself. She laughed as he approached crying, "You think you can defeat me! I am greater than an ugly insect like you could ever imagine!"

Raktavija, however, was an ancient demon of considerable powers, and as Kali attacked him furiously she found that each drop of his blood she spilt gave birth to a thousand more monsters.

"So," the gigantic demon said, "You see I am not so easily defeated." He roared with joy as she cut his arm and twenty-five thousand demons were spawned immediately clamoring for battle.

The world seemed full of the demonic force. Everywhere the demons raged and the gods blinked in shock and horror at the violent bloodshed, none of which seemed to lead anywhere. Shiva, Kali's husband, looked on from within his burning

Above: The goddess Kali seated on the double corpse of Shiva,
19th century, Punjab.

circle of flames, where he danced eternally, encircling the world order. Even he could not see Kali able to withstand this force of evil, so he stepped out of his burning orb towards her.

Kali lashed her enormous tongue and licked a drop of Raktavija's blood. A surge of demons were born within her and then destroyed by her immortal essence which consumes all. She rolled her great eyes and moved closer to the demon, lashing with her many swords, spitting words of power which could not be uttered by any other immortal. The demon shrank back as she smote his leg and then with her great tongue licked up his vile blood. Raktavija felt his power weakening and tried to escape, but Kali now had the taste for blood and pursued him relentlessly. By drinking all the blood of the giant demon, Kali was able to defeat him and his demonic multitudes.

Victorious, Kali emitted a deep sound which echoed through the universe, and all who heard it shuddered. Jumping upon the dead body she began to dance with joy, leaping and twirling until the whole galaxy quaked. Shiva, her husband, Lord of the Dance, called her to stop, but Kali, appearing not to hear, spun on and on.

"Kali! Cease this dance! Stop!" cried Shiva, for whom the worlds turned on their axes throughout the universe.

Again Shiva commanded his wife to stop, for the sacred madness of her dance threatened the fabric of all being, all order. But Kali danced on, her eyes and ears numbed to all but the dance. When Shiva approached her, he too was absorbed by her powerful dancing and soon lay beneath her pounding feet. The order of existence whirled and spun in fiery circles as she danced.

"Maha-Kali, Kali-Ma! Mother!" Shiva called in desperation, feeling his essence breaking down by the sheer power of this great, heaving goddess.

At once Kali listened. "Someone calls me, Mother. Kali-Ma, Mother." She slowed her dance and heard the cry again from under her turning feet.

Right: Indian painting of Kali in her wrathful aspect, 19th century.

95

Above: Indian painting of Kali dancing on Shiva, 18th century.

"Mother! Kali-Ma!"

"Surely a monster, a demon, cannot speak my sacred name," she thought. Then horror and shame struck into her heart as she saw under her dancing feet, her husband, Shiva, covered with the dreadful blood of the monsters. She lifted him in her mother's arms. Crooning with tenderness and sorrow, she cleaned and comforted him.

"Sweet Lord, I did not hear you," she said, rocking him in her arms. With infinite tenderness she placed Shiva, beloved

Lord, in the great burning circle where he held the order of
the universe. Shiva gazed into the dark eyes of Kali the kind,
Kali the terrible, Kali the absolute, and felt his essence
illuminate with understanding. Between them passed an
intense look, a shudder of complete joy, and bliss permeated
Shiva and the universe that day and forever.

Because of this story, Kali is entreated as the Great
Mother who will always hear the true cry from the deep heart
of any of her children.

Kuan Yin

China

In a world where qualities of compassion and mercy are rare, Kuan Yin holds out her willow branch of love. Her gentle presence is most keenly felt where there are rocks, willows, lotus pools or waters of any kind. Kuan means earth and Yin means woman.

Kuan Yin, goddess of compassion, Mother of Mercy, was the most popular goddess in China and surrounding countries, and is still widely worshiped today. Her Japanese manifestation is called Kwannon. Kuan Yin is portrayed as an exquisitely lovely woman, whose chief attribute is her boundless compassion. Utterly free from pride, ambition or vengefulness, she is the complete opposite of a wrathful god and is thought to be reluctant to punish even the wicked.

Fisher-folk love her dearly, and many depict her standing in a floating lotus, or gazing out to sea, holding the dew of compassion in a vase encircled by her arm. Images of Kuan Yin

Right: Marble statue of Kuan Yin, goddess of Mercy, Tang dynasty, 618–906 AD.

riding a dolphin or a great fish place her origins much earlier than the circa 100 AD some scholars quote as her beginnings. The Great Mother of early China was called Nu Kwa, and was sometimes portrayed as fish-tailed. When Buddhism entered China in 560 BC, worship of the Mother was already very old. She was loved to such an extent, she survived Buddhism by being absorbed into that belief system as Kuan Yin. According to the Buddhists, Kuan Yin is actually a perfected male Buddha who decided to incarnate as a woman in order to become a great spiritual teacher.

The following story is typical, showing Kuan Yin's essential goodness and purity. Among ten thousand other deities in the Orient, Kuan Yin alone remains the merciful goddess of compassion. This story was brought to China between 384–417 AD

MYTH OF KUAN YIN

Long ago in China lived a wealthy man who had no sons. A leader of strong, determined nature, he became governor of a certain province. When his wife gave birth to a baby girl, he was overjoyed and became greatly attached to his daughter, Mioa Shan. As she grew, Mioa Shan became as good as she was beautiful and kind to all she encountered. Mioa Shan was perfection to behold. The governor feared for her safety in an immoral world, and was unbending in the rules and regulations he set for her — Mioa Shan grew up virtually a prisoner in her own home. The walls around the great house were high, and she rarely had an opportunity to glimpse the outside world. When Mioa Shan did meet strangers who came to visit the governor on official business, she was serene and self-contained, though she longed to ask them about the world and the different places they had seen.

One spring day, Mioa Shan stood at the window of her chamber and gazed through the peach orchard in full bloom. But today she was not seeing the blossoms or the riotous colors of the flowers in the garden below, she was staring at a nearby hill on which stood an imposing monastery.

"I wonder what the monks do in that holy place?" she said. Her mother, who was passing by, answered, "Don't fill your head with such nonsense and wonderings. Come, child, we have silks to choose for your next embroidery."

Her mother's swift change of the subject did not go unobserved, for Mioa Shan had already noticed how her parents avoided her questions about the monastery. Even the servants were almost rude when she asked them such questions, questions for which they would surely know the answers, since they came from the nearby villages. Such rudeness to the daughter of the household was considered unthinkable — it was almost as though her father had given instructions for such questions not to be answered.

"I wonder what rites and ceremonies are performed by those saintly ones who live there?" Mioa Shan mused. She had a natural instinct for ceremony, and loved to arrange flowers in the garden temple. Or she would stand breathless before the stream which tumbled through the meadow beside the orchard.

"I would love to go to a big ceremony to give thanks for everything in this wonderful world." Mioa Shan knew as surely as the day follows night, that all manifestations in this world came from spirit. She knew that mountains, rocks and streams are as much living beings as birds and animals. A yearning to visit the monastery grew within her until it could be borne no longer. Mioa Shan was shy and modest, but had inherited enough of her father's determination to act when her mind was made up. Early one morning when everyone in the house was about their business, Mioa Shan

Above: Bronze statue of Kuan Yin, Ming dynasty.

slipped out, hurried past the kitchen where the servants were at breakfast, and out of the rarely used side gate. As she went along the path which led through the meadow and up the hill she felt elated and excited. "I will observe the religious ones at prayer and at their rites, and then I will creep home," she told herself firmly, a little breathless by the time she reached the monastery.

The gateway was opened by the gatekeeper who perceived her to be a young noblewoman, perhaps one who would give generously to the sadly lacking coffers. He ushered Mioa Shan into the shrine hall. Here she stood transfixed before

the statues of the Three Pure Ones, the central Trinity of Taoist deities. From within the monastery came the chanting of sacred songs. Mioa Shan felt certain she had come to a place of great holiness, and her pure heart rejoiced.

What Mioa Shan did not know was that the monastery had fallen into disrepute and was now a place of vice. Few truly holy men resided within its walls. Many monks spent their time fighting, drinking, gambling, and by night passed their time with village girls of fallen virtue. Certain she would

Below: Kuan Yin as goddess of Mercy, K'ang Hsi period (1662–1722).

be safe to wander around, Mioa Shan ventured up a dimly lit corridor. Three men in long monks robes overpowered her, stifled her screams and pulled her into a nearby alcove.

Meanwhile the governor, finding his beloved daughter gone, flew into a panic as he sent servants scurrying to find her. All day they searched, and it was late afternoon when a messenger came, saying that Mioa Shan had been seen entering the monastery. The governor's panic grew into rage. Without stopping to consider that his daughter might be a prisoner at the monastery, the governor assumed the worst. His mind filled with images of Mioa Shan in the arms of one of the vile hermits whose dissipated habits were legendary. He called for one hundred archers armed with burning torches to proceed at once to the hill top and surround the place of evil. "Destroy the monastery! Let nothing living be saved," the governor commanded.

The first burning arrow fell on the wooden outhouse. Fire quickly spread as the building was mostly constructed of lacquered wood. The villagers huddled in their houses as the fire on the hill top raged, a hideous torch for all to see. Not one human or creature escaped the blaze. Those who attempted to escape were shot down by a rain of arrows.

Determined to adhere to his usual routine, and not to show any of the mixed feelings churning within him, the governor took his normal walk in the peach orchard the next morning. Suddenly before him appeared a shimmering manifestation of Mioa Shan. She said, "Father, though you had no pity on me when I was an innocent girl held against my will, I have compassion in my heart for you. For you now have no daughter, and I have decreed that childless you will remain. Last night my plight was seen by merciful heaven and a glorious rainbow was sent to lift me above the flames, still pure and undefiled."

A rainbow shimmered above her head as she spoke and seemed to encircle her. More faintly she uttered the words

which were forever engraved into his wretched heart: "I have been made a goddess and I go now to join the immortals. My task will be always to comfort those in peril or afflicted by sorrow. I will watch over all beings and bless those who do not give in to rage, but live in kindness and love towards each other. From now on I shall be known as Kuan-Shi-Yin, Hearer-of-the-Cries-of-the-World."

In that moment the heart of the governor was opened. Tears pouring down his parched cheeks, he fell upon the ground crying, "Oh Mioa Shan, Kuan Yin. My daughter, how I have harmed you. I have been so wrong."

All at once the governor saw what a harsh and warlike life he had led. He resolved to live by the kindly dictates of his daughter, and to henceforward tell her story, that she might be ever remembered for her purity and goodness.

Leda

Greek

L eda represents the ancient connection of the Goddess to the bird, the egg and creation. Leda may have been another name for the goddess Lat who was believed to have hatched the World Egg. Some say she was really the goddess Nemesis who was also ravaged by Zeus (Jupiter). The complexity of the myths associated with Leda and her children would indicate she had some important standing in pre-Hellenic times (2500–1500 BC). However, the layering of Greek myths over Leda's original story which portrays her as a mother of mortals and immortals, makes it impossible to determine exactly how much. Prehistoric statues dating back to c.14 000 BC portray the Goddess as a pregnant bird. The story of Leda and the Swan has been a favorite source of inspiration to artists throughout the ages.

MYTH OF LEDA

The river Eurotas swirled around the beautiful body of Leda, wife of the King of Sparta. It was a secluded spot, much favored by Leda for her morning bathing.

"Leave me," she ordered the servant. "Come back in a little while."

Luxuriating in the soft water, she wanted to be alone, to feel the water making intimate little eddies around her legs

Right: Leda depicted with her two sets of twins and with Zeus as the swan. LEDA AND THE SWAN, *Francesco Melzi/Melzo (1439–1570).*

*Above: Leda and the swan, Roman wall painting, Herculanum, Italy,
1st century AD in the style of the 4th century BC.*

and hands, free to think. Her mind was on her husband and the night of love they had spent just a few hours ago. Tyndareus was brave and strong, the thought of his battle-scarred limbs entwined with hers sent a frisson of pleasure right to her fingertips. A smile played at the corner of her mouth, for she knew, in the way of women, that she had conceived and was with child.

High above in the heavens, the far-seeing eye of Zeus fell upon Leda bathing naked in the river. Her beauty and reverie held him captivated, and in that same moment he resolved to deceive her. A plan began to form within his mind and he quickly persuaded the goddess Aphrodite to take the form of a golden eagle with a cruel curved beak and talons.

"To amuse you," he said, "I will assume the body of this poor white bird." All at once he stood before her as a beautiful white swan, glorious, but no fighter. "Follow me! Pursue me," he dared, and Aphrodite, entering into the game in delight, took flight, swooping and darting at the swan who was great Zeus himself.

When they flew to the turn of the river Eurotus, Zeus called to Aphrodite, "Now, when I fall, leave me to my sport."

Watching Zeus the swan spiral downwards into the water just near the bathing Leda, Aphrodite saw the object of his game and resolved not to forget Zeus's insult. She snapped shut her cruel beak and turned back to Mount Olympus, while a curse fell upon the union which was about to occur below her.

The splash beside Leda made her gasp in alarm, and her hands flew to cover her nakedness. However, when she saw how exhausted the bird was, its snowy neck flecked with blood, her sympathies were engaged. High above she saw the wheeling eagle and thought she understood the plight of the fallen swan.

Above: LEDA AND THE SWAN, *Paul Tillier, (born c. 1934).*

"Poor bird", Leda said soothingly, stroking his ruffled feathers. "Poor, beautiful bird." She bathed his wounds with the cool waters of the river, talking to him all the while. She laid her cheek against his head. He trembled at her gentle caresses and sheltered in her arms, eventually laying his snowy head on her breast.

Suddenly all gentleness was gone. The great swan lifted himself up and grasped Leda to him, smothering her fearful protests with the feathers she had a moment before been caressing. The rape of Leda was swift and cruel. He left her sobbing in the waters, and did not look back.

When the servant returned a very different scene greeted her. Leda lay crouched on the river bank, crying in great distress.

"Your Majesty!" Leda's maid cried, rushing forward with a robe. "What has happened to you?"

But her mistress couldn't speak. Making all haste they returned to the palace, where Leda retired to her chamber, closing the door behind her.

Some say it was that same night as Leda lay with Tyndareus that she was beset with great birth pains. As dawn streaked the sky she laid a great egg. Two sets of twins were then hatched, two females, two males, two immortals and two mortals. Helen, whose legendary beauty was later to be cited as the cause of the fall of Troy, and Pollux were said to be the immortals, the children of Zeus. Clytamnestra, who became the wife of Agamemnon, and Castor were claimed to be the mortal children of the King of Sparta.

Leda's grief and despair so moved the gods that she was lifted up to heaven, where she was transformed and absorbed into Nemesis, the goddess of revenge. Nemesis's power was so great that she could avenge wrongdoing, not only during earthly lifetimes but in the foreverafter as well. Portrayed as a winged figure, representing divine anger, she moved relentlessly over land or sea, or turned the Wheel of Fate in favor of the good and in fury against the wicked.

Medea

Greece

M edea was a powerful sorceress, like Circe (see page 48), and was a granddaughter of the sun god Helios (Sol). In ancient times, before Greek mythology, Medea was said to be a fount of feminine healing. Her powers were so great that she could control the movements of the moon, sun and the stars. Medea is related to Metis, Titan mother of Athena (Minerva), who existed before the Olympic gods, and also the serpent goddess Medusa. Medea's name "Wise One" is derived from the Sanskrit word medha which describes the concept of "female wisdom".

MYTH OF MEDEA

Long ago lived Medea, princess of Colchis, a kingdom famous for its Golden Fleece. Protected by a fierce dragon, this magical Golden Fleece conveyed great powers and sovereignty upon its owner. The Greek hero Jason, a favorite of the goddess Hera, was seeking the Golden Fleece. High on Mount Olympus, Hera looked down on Jason and decided to help him.

Hera entreated Aphrodite, goddess of love, to aid her cause by making Medea fall in love with Jason. News of Medea's powerful witchcraft had even reached the heavens, and Hera knew that once Medea had been enticed to love

Right: Medea considering the murder of her children, Roman wall painting, Pompeii, 1st century.

Jason, she would use her magic to secure his way to the Golden Fleece, and allow him to bring it home to Greece.

So it was that Medea on seeing Jason fell desperately in love. Her father King Aietes had no intention of allowing the Golden Fleece to be surrendered to Jason, for the king knew that the sovereignty of his whole culture as separate from Greece was held within that sacred fleece. Once it was gone, so too were the old ways. For this reason the king had placed the fire-breathing dragon at the mouth of the cave which held the Golden Fleece. He spoke with Jason and the Argonauts, eventually placing the following conditions before him.

"I have no grudge against brave men. You can take the Golden Fleece if you accomplish these perilous tasks. First you must kill the dragon.

Above: Medea killing one of her sons, Italian vase painting found at Cumae, 340–320 BC.

Next, plough the field beside the dragon's cave and sow it with the dragon's teeth. From the dragon's teeth will spring fierce warriors, which you must also defeat. Only then," concluded King Aietes, "may you carry away the Golden Fleece."

Unbeknown to her father, Medea had whispered to Jason to come to her chamber. When he entered that dark room he shuddered, more afraid than he had been in many a bloodthirsty battle. It seemed this beautiful, yet fearsome woman somehow had a place in his future which even now cast a shadow over him like the cold of fingers reaching from the grave.

"Come Jason, I will help you." She spoke in a low voice, trembling with passion. "I have formed an inexplicable affection for you and I am at your service from this day forward."

Jason bent in a low bow and, it seemed, the goddess Hera whispered in his ear. "Trust Medea. Take her help. Later you can leave her behind. Take a proper wife later. Found a great house in your name."

Medea instructed Jason to strip off his clothing. Onto his body she smoothed an ointment that felt as cold on his naked skin as the iciest of north winds in winter. "This magic ointment will make you immune to the fire which shoots from the dragon's mouth. Go, kill the monster, and proceed in the sowing of the dragon's teeth. When the warriors spring from the earth, there will be too many for you to fight, for the dragon has many teeth."

"What shall I do?" the hero asked, shivering despite himself.

"Throw a stone among them," Medea replied. "They will become disturbed and confused and will fight each other. Take up the Golden Fleece in your arms and do not let it go until you are safely away from Colchis."

She looked at his disquieted face. He stared into her unfathomable dark eyes. He said, "Come with me, powerful and clever princess, for with you by my side I will be invincible."

She agreed, already a traitor to her own land, her own culture and her training in the ways of the goddess from time out of mind. Again Jason bowed low as he kissed her hand with its long tapering fingers. "All shall happen as you have told it," he said, and strode bravely forth to slay the dragon and overcome the dreadful tasks King Aietes had placed before him.

When Jason returned the Golden Fleece was flung proudly around his shoulders. Medea awaited with her brother

whom they took with them on her insistence. The people of Colchis gave chase, and without emotion Medea slew her brother and cut his body into several pieces which she threw along the road as they traveled. Their pursuers stopped to pick up the pieces of their prince for burial, thus giving Jason, Medea and the Argonauts time to escape.

After more adventures, during which Medea had again and again used her astonishing and brutal magic to the benefit of Jason, they arrived in Corinth where the travelers were given a royal welcome. Jason was lauded as a great warrior and hero, and the Golden Fleece brought him the fame and sovereignty he had craved. For Medea, however, Jason felt nothing but gratitude. He kept her in a large house outside the city, never allowing her to be part of his everyday life. Still enchanted by Aphrodite's spell, Medea gave Jason two fine sons and remained faithful and loving to him, content with whatever time he spared for her. Ever ambitious, Jason longed for a respectable bride who would provide the right name for his two sons. He became engaged to Glauce, the daughter of the king of Corinth, in order to start a dynasty in his name.

Hearing news of Jason's plans, Medea threw herself on her bed weeping tears of grief and abandonment. She had done so much for Jason. She had given up her home and used her magic to his benefit against her own kinsmen. Suddenly the spell upon her broke, and Medea saw what she had done for a love which had never been returned. "I have been cursed by my love for this man! Love! Love! It is death to love like this, without reason, without his earning my love. I am shamed by this love," she cried, as the illusion fell from her eyes and she saw her own responsibility in all that had happened.

Left: Medea and her children, Roman wall painting from Pompeii, 1st century.

Medea, her face terrible in its grief, raised up her voice to the old ways, to the Great Mother she had served always before she had fallen into this entrapment. "By the ancient Goddess I shall be avenged," she said, and summoned with her hand of fire, the winged chariot drawn by serpents to hurtle towards her from the center of the heavens.

"First," she whispered, "the princess Glauce."

Lifting up her arms in a fearsome gesture, Medea uttered an incantation of words, the power of which caused the candles to gutter and die in their holders. There, manifested on the floor, was a magnificent bridal gown of exquisite design and fabric. Medea picked up the gown and deftly smoothed a magic potion into its lining., Medea called to her servant and instructed her to carry this wedding gift to the princess. When Glauce saw the gown shimmering in the arms of Medea's servant, she immediately grasped the gown to her breast and decided to try it on. Never had she seen such a garment, it was perfection.

But as Glauce fastened the final clasp her screams rent the air. She was ensnared in the fiery garment, and by the time her maidservant had opened the door, Glauce was burned to ash inside the still magnificent, undamaged dress lying on the floor.

Back at her house, Medea watched all that happened on the cloudy surface on her bowl of prophesying water. When she saw the horrible end of her rival, she laughed, and gathering her cloak about her she whistled low to her winged chariot drawn by its flying serpents.

Sadly, she looked at her beloved sons, cherubic in sleep. "And now, you," she whispered, using the thou address.

Her mouth was like a blood-red flower, its petals beginning to drop like a scarlet carpet at her bare feet. Some say that she killed her sons at once, and some say she called upon the goddess Hera who had caused her all this pain, to take care of them.

Above: Medea killing her children, from the French translation of
The Book of Famous Women *by Giovanni Boccaccio, 15th century.*

Whatever the outcome, Jason never saw his bride-to-be, Medea or his children again. He died a broken man after wandering aimlessly through Greece for many years. Medea, in respect for her great witchcraft, flew straight to the Elysian Fields after she left the earth plane. There she became a goddess and came to be worshiped in Italy as the snake divinity Angita.

Pandora

Greece

Originally Pandora was a goddess who held a honey vase, not a box, from which she poured blessings, not ills. Goddesses of old were known to hold vessels which were womb-like, from which life-enhancing forms would flow. In ancient texts Pandora was called "the sender-forth-of-gifts", the "All-giver" and was thought to be a manifestation of the earth goddess Rhea. As Greek society changed, Pandora was depicted as an Eve figure who brought all evils into the world.

Hesiod, the Greek poet, recorded the story of Pandora (700 BC). In the following myth, the vase is used instead of the "box" to tell the story of Pandora.

MYTH OF PANDORA

There was a time when it was said that no woman had yet been created and only man existed. Zeus (Jupiter), who was angry with the Titan called Prometheus and his brother Epimetheus for stealing the fire from the heavens and giving it to man, plotted to send them a gift which would cause them much trouble. This trouble was to be in the form of a beautiful woman, the first of her sex.

Zeus called upon the god of crafts, Hephaestus (Vulcan), to fashion a woman, and asked Athena (Minerva) to breathe soul into that creation. Thus Zeus created Pandora in

Right: PANDORA, *Dante Gabriel Rossetti (1828–1882).*

120

Above: EVA PRIMA PANDORA, *Jean Cousin the Elder (c. 1490–c. 1560)*
Pandora is pictured here with a sacred vase or vessel.

loveliness and called on all the gods to add gifts to her that she may be complex and beautiful. Aphrodite gave her charm; Apollo gifted her with music, sweet and sure; Hermes added his gift of persuasion and great curiosity, and all the other gods and goddesses added their gifts. Richly prepared, Pandora was given the ancient, sacred vessel of a honey vase which had been known in the times when the goddess reigned supreme in all worlds, as the cornucopia or horn of plenty.

Zeus emptied the vessel of all its life-giving abundance and placed within it evil and pestilence: war, famine, disease, anger, jealousy, envy and greed were just a few of the horrors he placed in the sacred vase. He then covered the top with a lid, which could only be prized free with some difficulty. This vessel, he told Pandora, must never be opened or great troubles would result for the world.

When Epimetheus saw Pandora, he was struck by her beauty and charms and received her gladly into his home. His brother Prometheus had reason to doubt the honesty of Zeus and warned Epimetheus to beware of Zeus and any gifts he may bring.

All seemed to be proceeding happily for the couple as Epimetheus was a good and kind husband, and Pandora was beautiful, meek and willing. There was within her, however, a memory which seemed to elude her whenever she tried to recall her life beyond Mount Olympus. This memory transported her to a time when she had been more powerful and had known much. When once more the memory eluded her, Pandora stretched and walked about the room.

"What was it now," she pondered, and her glance fell on the tightly closed honey vase. Searching her mind, it was to Pandora like a beach swept clean by the night waves, with no imprint left to guide her. She fingered the vase. How good it

felt, how smooth, how like her own body in shape the way it rose and fell, swelled in and out. The more Pandora observed the vessel, the more she felt sure the answer to her loss of memory was inside it. Her curiosity stirred. Why had Zeus told her not to lift the lid? Why had he been so adamant about it? Her own half-remembered truth told her that the vase had once brought wonderful, not terrible, things into the world. She felt perplexed, frustrated at the blankness of her own mind; then she resolved to look inside. Quickly she lifted down the vase and with strong, deft movements she struggled to loosen the tight lid. At once it was loose in her hand and from the vessel came a vile buzzing sound, then out flew hideous shapes. Demons and devils flew about cackling and screeching at her:

"Pandora, you have been tricked! Now we are free to bring woe to the world."

Pandora dropped the vessel, her heart pounding. Fear caused her hands to tremble. How could this be? Her memory was that the vase held good things. As if from far away she heard the sound of a woman crooning a lullaby. The words were hard to catch, but she knew they came from some time before Zeus, before this trickery and deception had befallen her. The woman's voice sang:

"Pandora, empty the vase. Pandora, seek again in the honey vase."

Mesmerized, Pandora lifted the vase again and shook it gently as if pouring from it the dregs. A strong, sweet scent rose to her nostrils, and a light and dreamy form drifted from the open mouth of the vase. It called to her as it circled her body.

"I am Hope," it said softly. " Zeus did not properly empty the vessel of the Great Mother before he placed the demons on top of me." Hope shook herself and shimmered, crying out,

"Oh, such an odor! Such a stench to have placed upon me!" She shuddered again, and said, "But I am here now, and I have much to do if I am to alleviate the suffering Zeus has intended for this poor world. Goodbye, and thank you for releasing me."

So saying, Hope flew out the window to spread her healing presence amid the horror which had been sent upon the earth.

Pandora sat in the dying light. She knew that she, woman, would be blamed for this monstrous happening, so she sealed a memory within herself which could be discovered by women of the future. It was the memory of feeling at one with a great feminine presence who filled her with belief in herself. Remembering this power in her own body, she had lifted the great cornucopia of life, and poured hope into the world.

Pele

Hawaii

Above: Wooden carving of Pele, the Hawaiian goddess of fire, 17th–18th century.

Of all the world's goddesses, Pele the Volcano Woman, is still actively worshiped by the people who live nearby her boiling crater in Hawaii. If the volcano grumbles and threatens eruption, villagers hurry to offer her gifts of silks, tobacco, special foods and decoctions of brandy. More than once she has stopped her lava flow just before engulfing the villages from which the offerings were made. Stories are told by visitors to Hawaiian volcanoes of meetings with an ancient woman who asks for a cigarette. It is said that by snapping her fingers she creates a fire from which she lights the cigarette, then in the wink of an eye she disappears. The local villagers nod sagely and say that Pele is roundabout and to beware. The following story is recorded from ancient times in oral traditions.

MYTH OF PELE

Pele was the daughter of the earth goddess, Haumea. She showed her attraction to fire when still very young, seeking it wherever she could. "Show me how you make fire." she would

ask of anyone she met. She learnt the different ways of creating a spark, and keeping a fire safe with smoldering ashes; she even learnt how to light a fire with wet wood. But it was the fire beneath the earth which most fascinated Pele. She yearned to go up to the once active great volcanoes on her island home. She listened to the stories which northerners and travelers told of great mountains which would suddenly open to reveal the fire deep within the earth. Her whole being strained to go there to see this mystery.

The sea goddess Namaka foretold that Pele would bring trouble to the land of her mother, who had kept the volcanoes nearby dormant. Nakama decided to watch her sister Pele closely. One dark night Pele crept up to the silent craters and began to dance the hula, winding her slow hips round and round. Faster she moved until she touched the fire in her belly and flicked it out from her fingertips, kindling the fires in the craters, which leapt to her call.

The eruptions that followed brought havoc upon the land her mother had created. Haumea, her mother, decided Pele should leave with some of her sisters to find a home of her own, for she knew the sea goddess would punish Pele if she stayed in her mother's land. They set off. Pele held out a divining rod to decide which of the small atolls would be good places for them to settle and build islands.

Nakama, still angry with the havoc Pele had created, followed the sisters as they traveled by canoe. As they came to the atoll which would become Hawaii, Nakama rose up from the sea to do battle with Pele. The great foes fire and water met in a tremendous brawl. As water is the stronger element, Pele was defeated and rose as vapor, disembodied. She floated up into the mountains to rekindle the energy of the volcanoes, making her home in her favorite, Kilauea.

The Hawaiian people came to respect and love Pele, making offerings nearby to her burning intensity. They believed she gave the people the gift of the home fire for cooking and for light, and that she was the essence of earthly fire. They spun myths and tales of Pele and her many lovers. It is said that when Pele and her lover argue, the volcanoes spit and hiss, but when they have a really major fight, the volcano erupts.

Psyche

Greek

Psyche's name means "soul". The myth of Psyche is a wonderful allegorical tale of the human heart, through which we can participate in the power and endurance of love.

This old story was first recorded by the second century AD Roman writer Apuleius in his work *The Golden Ass*.

MYTH OF PSYCHE AND EROS (CUPID)

Long ago in the west of Greece lived a king who had three beautiful daughters. The elder two were of more than common beauty, but the youngest daughter, whose name was Psyche, was so lovely that words cannot describe her. When strangers saw her they were struck speechless. However graceful her body, it was Psyche's face which engaged the onlooker, with its sweetness and serenity. Word of Psyche's beauty spread and admirers came from near and far to catch a glimpse of her. Soon men began to praise her, saying she was more beautiful than Aphrodite, queen and goddess of beauty. Bedazzled by Psyche, men began to neglect the shrines of the great Aphrodite. Flowers withered in their jars on the altars and the shrines remained unswept and unattended. Aphrodite was infuriated by the news of the interloper, who claimed her place in the hearts and imaginations of men, and plotted to depose her rival.

Above: Psyche is often depicted as a butterfly which represents the soul's flight towards freedom. PSYCHE, *Charles Frederick Lowcock (1878–1922)*

Above: PSYCHE SHOWING HER SISTERS HER GIFTS FROM CUPID,
Jean-Honore Fragonard (1732–1806).

Aphrodite called for her son Eros. She ordered him to
create mischief for Psyche, by causing her to fall in love with a
miserable and ugly creature. Eros made himself invisible and
entered Psyche's bed chamber where he found her asleep.
Bending over her, Eros pierced himself with one of his own
arrows and fell deeply in love with her.

Psyche, cursed by Aphrodite, experienced swings of joy
and despair. Her less beautiful sisters had easily found
husbands and had left the palace. She was left with
dumbfounded admirers who strew her path with flowers, but

could not speak to her. Psyche took to sitting alone in her chamber, tears of misery streaming down the perfect cheeks she had begun to hate.

The king and queen began to fear for Psyche and took her to a famed oracle to ask about the fate of their daughter. The oracle spoke:

"Your daughter is fated never to be the bride of any mortal lover. She is destined to be the wife of a monster, so fierce that men and gods quake before him. This monster lives on the top of a mountain. Your daughter must go there directly."

Though her parents wept profusely at this terrible utterance, Psyche remained calm and serene. "I am resigned to my fate, so take me to it," she said.

They set off to the high mountain and left Psyche shivering and tearful amid the towering rocks. "Was it my fault that men said I was a goddess, more beautiful than Aphrodite?" she asked the wind. As if by answer Zephyrus (Favonius), the west wind, lifted her up and carried her to a leafy glade where he laid her down and she fell asleep.

Waking, Psyche saw a delightful palace. She felt drawn into it, as every curve in the arches, every carving in the roof seemed to whisper her name. So beautiful a building must have been created by a godly hand, she thought. She wandered through the lovely rooms, engaged by the outlook, admiring the furnishings, when she heard a voice speak her name.

"Most fair queen," the voice said, "this palace and everything in it is yours. Speak an order and it shall be carried out by us your invisible servants. Upstairs in your own suite of rooms a bath has been prepared in readiness for your arrival. If you are hungry, sit at the table and ask for whatever you desire and it shall be immediately given."

All was just as the invisible voice had pronounced, and Psyche bathed and ate sumptuously, before resting on her bed.

That night her bridegroom came. He felt like no monster, with his smooth cheeks and thighs and tender passion. However, before dawn each day he was gone. Psyche implored him to reveal himself to her.

"Psyche," he said "Though I love you more than life itself, I cannot show myself to you. I beg you do not ask to see my face."

Left: Marble statue of Cupid and Psyche, Antonio Canova (1757–1822).

"I love you too, dear husband," Psyche said. "I will try to stop asking you, though it is very difficult."

Psyche passed the days in the woods or amused herself in the palace, but she grew more and more lonely of spirit with each passing day. She begged her husband to allow her sisters to come and visit her, and he agreed. Zephyrus, the god of the west wind, went immediately and carried Psyche's sisters to the palace where they embraced her, telling her all the news from home. Psyche invited them inside the beautiful palace and ordered food for her guests. It magically appeared on golden plates and was so delicious that the sisters began to feel the demon jealousy prick them. When Psyche called for music to entertain her sisters, a lute began to play, filling the room with delight.

"Where is your husband?" sister number one asked, thinking how poor her own castle seemed, how dull the table, how the rooms never resounded with music.

"Oh," Psyche said, lying, "he is away on business. He is a merchant who travels frequently."

"But," sister number two said, "he must be very rich to keep such a magnificent palace."

Eventually Psyche confided in her sisters that she had never seen her husband.

"What! You have never seen him," they cried in unison. "He may be a monster with two heads!"

Together they urged Psyche to spy on her husband by taking a lamp into the bedroom and lighting it when he was asleep. They said, "Carry a knife, for remember the prediction from the oracle which said you would marry a monster. Before the monster awakes, cut off his head."

Against her inner knowing, Psyche did as her sisters had suggested, and soon she held the lamp aloft over the sleeping body of her husband. Psyche gasped, for there before her was the most beautiful young man, with long, strong limbs and

Above: THE STORY OF CUPID AND PSYCHE, *Jacopo del Sellaio (1441/42–1493).*

the most glorious face she had ever seen. From his shoulders grew two dewy wings, as soft as swan's down. It was Eros the god of love himself. So this was the monster the oracle had predicted, the one most feared by gods and men, for his arrows rendered all as helpless as babies. She lifted the lamp higher, when three drops of burning oil dropped his chest. Eros cried out in pain and confusion.

When he saw Psyche, he leapt from the bed saying sadly, "Psyche could you not trust me? I have gone against my mother's wishes to be with you. I must leave you, and that will be your punishment. Love cannot exist where there is no trust." So saying, he flew out the window, and Psyche fell in a dead faint of grief.

When Psyche awoke she found the palace had disappeared

and she was alone in a field not far from where her sisters and parents lived. Psyche felt the quickening of new life within her, and tears began to flow anew.

"I must go to my sisters to tell them this terrible news," she thought. The sisters listened, pretending sympathy while inwardly rejoicing at their sister's misfortune. Both were thinking that they would leave their husbands and go to the beautiful palace and offer themselves to the god Eros in place of Psyche. But when they each called the wind Zephyrus to lift them to the palace, his strong arms were not there to catch them and the two sisters dropped to be dashed to pieces on the rocks below.

Poor Psyche wandered in search of her love, eating little, but her beauty, instead of withering, grew more and more.

She approached all she met begging for news of Eros, until she came at last to entreat Aphrodite, his mother, to restore Eros to her.

Aphrodite, confronting Psyche in her growing loveliness, was enraged and set Psyche a series of near-impossible tasks. First she had to sort overnight a room filled with a mixture of seeds. She accomplished this with the help of the humble ants who came to her aid. Next Psyche was told to gather the sun-sheep's fleece, though they were fierce and deadly. She cried out to the stream, and the spirit of the waters assisted her by instructing her to gather the fleece as it stuck to the briars and trees. Lastly, Aphrodite commanded Psyche to go to the underworld and bring back the secret of eternal beauty in a closed box.

The last assignment proved too difficult for Psyche to resist even though she was assisted by an unseen voice which helped her reach the underworld unharmed. When Persephone, queen of the underworld, had given her the tightly closed box, Psyche's strength weakened. She was within sight of the entrance to the underworld when she stopped.

"I am so tired," she thought, "and Aphrodite will never be satisfied. She will think of more and more terrible tasks for me. I might as well just take a peek inside this box, so that I may have a little more beauty to please my husband, when I find him."

She pushed aside the warning of the unseen voice: "Psyche, do not look inside the box. It is not for a mortal woman to pry into the secrets of divine beauty."

Unheeding, she opened the lid and peeped inside. Nothing was there except a strange odor, but then she was beset by an overwhelming desire to sleep. The darkness engulfed her and soon she lay as dead on the side of the road.

In that moment strong arms enfolded her. Hands swept the sleep of death from her and enclosed it once more within

the box. Two warm lips breathed the life back into her. A voice seemed to come from far away:

"Wake up, my dear love," Eros said. "We will return this box to my mother, then I am taking you on a journey."

Eros had resolved to make application to great Zeus (Jupiter) that he and his beloved Psyche be married. Psyche felt herself lifted up into the heavens until they stood before Zeus on his throne. Eros stated his case and Zeus deliberated.

"You have caused me much mischief, boy," he said. "You have caused me to change into all manner of creatures, like swans and horses! All for love and lust too many times." Zeus slapped this broad thigh, threw back his great head and laughed.

"But, by all the gods it was fun and I would not be without you, nor have you unhappy. You may marry your Psyche who shall live here on Mount Olympus as the goddess she truly has become."

Lightning flashed and shattered the air in splinters of light. A great feast was held on Mount Olympus, and all the divinities witnessed the joining of hands of the lovers, Psyche and Eros. After so many trials they were joined in perpetual happiness, never to grow old, but to live in lasting bliss with their children, Joy and Youth.

Sekhmet

❖

Egypt

Before recorded time, Sekhmet in her half-lioness form moves over the scorched sands of Egypt. Like the Sphinx, enigmatic in the desert, her face has been blurred by time and almost forgotten. Sekhmet is one of the most ancient deities known to the human race, her origin before Egypt unknown. She is a reminder of that period when gods and goddesses were witness to the beginning of time.

By the time myths were being recorded in writing, Sekhmet was called the daughter of Ra the sun god, leader of the Egyptian gods. Early goddesses all had a terrible aspect, and they could exist as both deities of love and war. Sekhmet has been called the "terrible" goddess of vengeance, war and retribution. In Egyptian mythology it was she who punished the damned in the underworld. However, she was also worshiped in her aspect of Great One of Healing, the setter of bones.

Left: Black granite statue of Sekhmet, the lion goddess, 18th dynasty.

138

Sekhmet has some 4000 names which describe her various aspects and qualities. In her aspect of sovereignty over the Tablets of Destiny, Sekhmet becomes a goddess of Fate, who holds the future of humanity in her hands.

She is the dark face of the mother goddess Hathor and the lover goddess Isis. Together they form the formidable faces of the triple goddess of ancient Egypt. This tale of Sekhmet comes from c.2000 BC.

MYTH OF SEKHMET

In ancient days humans had become contemptuous of the gods. They warred and they squabbled. They neglected to worship. "Why should we pray to the gods?" they said. "We are as good as gods ourselves. Look at our magnificent buildings! Look at our weapons! Look at our jewels and gold! We have created laws. We have no need to bow down to any god or abide by god-given laws."

So they turned their backs on the gods who had given them life. They even swore against the sun god, Ra.

"We shall learn the words of power, by masquerading as god fearing," the men of the temples said in low voices. "We will listen hard. Once we have learned the words of power, we shall utter them and become gods ourselves." In this way they plotted to overthrow Ra and his pantheon.

The great Ra, who traveled the world each day, heard the plans and schemes. He called a meeting of the gods to devise a way to stop the rebellion on earth. On his head, behind the eye of the raised serpent, glittered the terrible Sekhmet. The gods, having discussed the situation, decided that Sekhmet should be the one to appear on earth to show the power of the gods and quash the uprising. Her loyalty and pledge to protect Ra from his enemies was well known and respected by all the gods. Her

Left: Stone relief of Sekhmet from Sebek and Horus Temple, Kom Ombo

antiquity was so great that even the gods didn't know from whence she had come. Yet they knew that nothing could withstand the force of Sekhmet, whose name means "Powerful".

Once unleashed, the terrible power of the goddess Sekhmet knew no bounds. She hurled forth upon the earth from the eye of Ra as an immense, fiery lioness, whose back glowed with the color of blood. She commenced a slaughter of the human race, the like of which had never been seen by gods or men. The gods tried to stop Sekhmet, but she had acquired the taste for human blood. She rejoiced in the killing. On and on she rampaged until the earth soaked red.

Ra called to her, raising his great arm: "Enough Sekhmet!" But she snarled at him, scarcely stopping for breath. "When I taste human blood, my heart rejoices," she said. "Great Ra, she must be stopped," the horrified gods cried. "Most ancient Sekhmet, goddess of force, must be restrained!"

Ra looked upon the carnage, much troubled. His daughter had far exceeded his wishes; if humanity were destroyed there would be no one to worship the gods. With no worshipers, the gods would become bored and fight among themselves. Words of power were of no use in dealing with Sekhmet in her rage and blood lust. He must find another way. Ra called to the god Sekti and instructed him to mix a potion of seven

thousand vats of beer mixed with the juice of the deep red pomegranate until it resembled human blood. The disguised beer was poured into a huge pool in the path of the marauding lioness. Ra hid, hoping she would mistake the liquid for the blood she craved. Sekhmet fell for the trick and lapped at the mixture until she fell down, intoxicated.

Some say that instead of rage, miraculously, the heart of Sekhmet was suddenly filled with joy. Some say she merely slept for a long time. Some say she was expressing the darkness within the mother goddess, Hathor. Some say she was showing the wildness of the benevolent cat goddess, Bast. What is known is that when she awoke all her rage was gone. Sekhmet stretched her long, warm limbs, yawned, showing her pink curling tongue, and began to purr, a slow, deep purr. She was content and never attacked humans again. However, to appease the goddess, before whose power even he had quaked, Ra decreed that henceforward the same intoxicating liquor was to be brewed on the feast day of Hathor each year.

"As many vats of beer as there are priestesses of the goddess," he decreed. In this ritual way, the greatness of Sekhmet was remembered.

Above: Pectoral (ornamental breastplate) depicting Ptah and the lion goddess Sekhmet.

Snake Goddess

Ancient cultures

The serpent or snake has long been associated with the goddess in many cultures, from pre-Hellenic Greece to the Australian Aboriginal creation serpent. A very ancient symbol, the uroborus depicts the snake creating a circle by biting its own tail. The body of the snake can be seen as a male image, its open mouth, the female. The uroborus shows that in the beginning neither male nor female was first, but rather both together created the whole. However, much evidence exists for early serpent imagery being predominantly female. In Africa peoples believed the snake taught women how to give birth by revealing its convulsive spasms when swallowing food. These were likened to birthing movements.

The serpent was seen as never aging, as being in a state of constant renewal and rebirth as it shed its skin over and over yet did not die. In Hindu myths the Great Mother was perceived as a serpent which remained coiled in the pelvis of humans as the kundalini energy. Through much spiritual practice, it was believed that a human could encourage the kundalini to uncoil and slowly move through the spinal chakras (seven energy centers of the body) until it burst through the top of the head as infinite wisdom. Ancient civilizations did not have the fear of snakes that modern ones do. Snakes were generally seen as life-enhancing, creative and healing animals filled with knowledge.

In ancient Greece the snake was believed to have a direct link with the earth goddess, and at certain sacred caves and temples priestesses would leave especially prepared honey cakes to feed the snakes. It was hoped that the snakes having eaten

Above: Ancient snake goddess figurine from Heraklion,
Knossos, Crete, c.1600 BC.

the cakes would take the messages and wishes invested in them to Gaia (Tellus) deep within the earth.

The ancient Chinese believed the mother of all divinities was a huge serpent called Mat Chinoi, who had a womb filled with angels. These angelic ones received the souls of the dead who needed to re-enter the body of the great serpent. Shamans had to undergo re-entry into the paradise belly of Mat Chinoi before they could be reborn as healers for the whole community. In ancient Palestine the great serpent was worshiped as Leviathon, the mate of the moon goddess. He became the enemy of Yahweh; the two gods battled together and, the story goes, they will battle again on doomsday. Much Gnostic literature speaks of the serpent bringing the "light of knowledge" to the people. Jung, the great twentieth century psychiatrist, when asked how he knew this amazing fact or that, was said to reply: "I know because my snake told me." He would then pat his pelvis, the place where the Indians believe the kundalini to reside.

In ancient Crete the snake and the goddess were inextricably interlinked. The Cretan culture was the inheritor of the goddess worshiping culture of Old Europe with its traditional connection between goddess and snake as far back as 6000 BC. Many statues were found depicting the goddess with snakes coiled around her body and held erect in her upraised hands in some sort of divine statement. What exactly was meant is lost to us, but the statues themselves are strong and evoke wonder in the viewer.

The Pelasgians were tribes mentioned by Homer, who inhabited Greece before the time of formal Greek history, that is earlier than 2500 BC. From the Pelasgians comes one of the earliest recorded myths of the Snake and the Goddess, the myth of Eurynome and Ophion. Pelasgus, or First Man referred to in the following myth, was said to be contemporary with the myth of the rape of Persephone (Proserpina).

MYTH OF EURYNOME

Pelasgian

Eurynome, Goddess of All Things, rose up naked from primordial Chaos. So that she might have somewhere to place her feet she began her works by dividing the sky from the waters. Joyously, Eurynome moved upon the undulating waves, causing a great wind to be created by her whirling dance. This wind began to swirl around Eurynome, curving to her divine being. She grasped this wind and, as they danced, rubbed it between her hands. As the wind rose and fell, coiling about her, a huge serpent was revealed and Eurynome named him Ophion. As Eurynome and the serpent moved, the dance became first sensual then erotic. The Goddess and the serpent coupled and Eurynome became pregnant.

Right: Figurine of the Minoan snake goddess from Knossos, Crete, 1600 BC.

145

Immediately after this Eurynome rose into the air, assuming the shape of a white dove. She flew rising and falling, swooping and swerving until she came to rest on the waters to brood, settling her divine feathers about her. In time she cried out and laid the Universal Egg into the great waters. Eurynome bade Ophion to coil himself seven times around the Egg until it hatched. Together they watched over the Egg. At last a mighty heaving started to vibrate from within it. Watching intently, the goddess and the serpent saw a jagged crack appear on the surface of the Egg. All things that exist soon tumbled out: the sun, moon, stars and all living creatures. Their work done, Eurynome and Ophion retired to their vantage point at the center of the universe on Mount Olympus to observe life below.

Ophion angered the goddess by his boastfulness, for he went about bragging that he alone was the creator of the universe. Eurynome was so angry that she seized the great serpent and hit him hard about the head, once, twice, ten times until nearly all his teeth fell out. Next she trampled Ophion under her heel and banished him forever to live in holes and caves beneath the earth.

Eurynome shaped the first man from the dropped teeth of Ophion mixed with the soil of Arcadia. His name was Pelasgus, ancestor of the Pelasgians, the aboriginal inhabitants of Greece. Other humans followed, fashioned by Eurynome's creative hand, and they banded together for warmth and comfort, living off acorns and various roots from the forest. Eurynome at last could rest, content that earthly matters had been correctly put in motion.

GLOSSARY

ANCIENT GREEKS: The first Greeks, revered for their intelligence and curiosity, were herders who came from the north about 2000 BC. They conquered the Pelasgian tribes who inhabited the territory now known as Greece. The Greeks traced their origins back to Thessaly and called themselves Hellenes after an early war-loving king, Hellen. The Greek war-loving nature gave rise to many conquests of land and sea, including Crete, and voyages to Italy and beyond. Myths were created about the conquest of Greece and the earliest of Greeks myths told of old gods fighting the new for supremacy. In time Zeus became the ruler of the Greek gods, though the old stories were still treasured. From this rich blend of mythology come the stories we have today.

ANCIENT ROMANS: T Tradition has it that Rome was founded in 753 BC and that the Romans overran Thessaly and Delphi in Greece in 280 BC. The Romans had vegetation and nature myths from the distant past, but no organized mythology of their own. They were so delighted with the complex and fascinating Greek folklore that they adopted the Greek gods and worshiped them as their own. Thus Zeus became Jupiter, Poseidon became Neptune, Aphrodite became Minerva, and so on.

APULEIUS: Roman author born 125 AD. He wrote important works such as *The Golden Ass*, in which Greek, Roman and some Egyptian myths are recorded.

BRONZE AGE: Signifies early human use of bronze, a

compound of nine parts copper and one part tin. Difficult to date as different cultures acquired the skill at various times. Started first in Egypt and Mesopotamia c.3000 BC, bronze implements and artefacts appeared in Crete around 2800 BC.

BYBLOS: (Modern Gebail) a port known to pre-dynastic Egypt. (3150–3050 BC) on coast of Phoenicia (modern Lebanon).

CRETE: Island site of the Minoan culture 3000 BC.

HESIOD: Greek poet believed to have been born around 700 BC. His greatest work was the Theogony, an important source on the lives of the gods.

HOMER: Greek poet and storyteller who is believed to have written the Iliad and the Odyssey, the original sources of most of the Greek myths. Homer was probably born in the ninth or tenth century BC; however, there are many estimates of his birth, all based on the time of the Trojan War which took place about 1184 BC.

ICE AGE: 35000 BC–9000 BC.

INANNA: The Sumerian goddess of heaven and earth. Her visit to the underworld is the earliest recorded myth of the goddess who descends to the regions of the dead (c. 2000 BC). On sending her husband Dumuzi to the underworld for three months of the year, during which she grieved, she established the vegetation cycles of winter and spring. Later, Babylonian gods Isthar and Tammuz, and the Greek myths of Aphrodite and Adonis, and Demeter and Persephone have their ancient echoes in her story.

ISHTAR: See Inanna

MOUNT OLYMPUS: The highest mountain of the Greek peninsular near the borders of Macedonia and Thessaly. Due to its great height (over 9000 feet), it

was believed to be the home of the gods, and so is important in mythology.

MYCENAEAN CIVILIZATION: Mycenaean civilization developed in the mainland of Greece in the Late Bronze Age from 1580–1120 BC. It came from the fusion of Greek genius, Cretan Minoan culture and imagination, and the inventiveness and skills of earlier inhabitants of Greece.

OVID: Roman poet (43 BC–17 AD) whose various works, including Metamorphoses, contain many of the Greco-Roman myths.

PELASGIAN: Pre-Hellenic peoples who inhabited Greece before the arrival of Bronze Age Greeks.

PHOENICIA: A group of city states between about 1200 and 1000 BC. This coastal area is now occupied by Lebanon and parts of Syria and Israel.

POSEIDON: The Greek god of the waters, the sea and of earthquakes. When Zeus divided up the world, the underworld was apportioned to Hades, the sky was reserved for himself, and Poseidon was given dominion over the earth and waters.

SUMER: South region of Babylonia; seat of a civilization in 3rd millennium BC.

ZEUS: The father-protector of all the Greek gods, his origin is Indo-European. Essentially a sky and weather god, his blessing was a clear sky and his weapon, the thunderbolt and the lightning strike. Zeus lived high in the mountains where the weather was uncertain, like his temper. Having overthrown his own father Cronos, Zeus established his supremacy among the remaining gods. He was long and unhappily married to the goddess Hera, but had many lovers and numerous offspring to both goddesses and mortal women.

HOW TO PRONOUNCE NAMES IN THIS BOOK

Actaeon	ak-Teeon	Isis	Eye-sis
Adonis	a-Donis	Ithaca	Ithaka
Aeaea	Ay-ay-a	Kali	Karli
Aphrodite	afra-Dyti	Knossos	Nossus
Apollo	a-Pollo	Kuan Yin	Kwan Yin
Ariadne	ari-Adni	Leda	Leeda
Artemis	Artimis or	Medea	me-Dear
	ar-Temis	Medusa	me-Dyou-za
Athena	Atheena	Metis	May-tis
Baubo	Bow-bo	Minoan	me-Nohwan
Byblos	Bib-loss	Minos	Min-os
Circe	Ser-see	Minotaur	Mina-tor
Clytemnestra	clytim-Nestra	Mioa Shan	Myow Shan
Crete	Creet	Mycenae	my-See-nee
Cronos	Cro-nos	Mycenaen	mysee-Neean
Cyprus	Sy-prus	Nemesis	Nemisis
Cythera	se-Theara	Nut	Noot
Daphne	Daf-nee	Odysseus	Odiss-us
Demeter	de-Meeta	Olympus	oh-Limpus
Devi	Dayvi	Ophion	Off-ion
Dionysus	dya-Nysus	Osiris	oh-Siris
Ephesus	Efisus	Pandora	pan-Dora
Epimetheus	epee-Meethus	Pelasgian	pe-Layz-jian
Erebus	Eribus	Pelasgus	pe-Layz-jus
Eros	Ear-os	Pelé	Pelay
Eurylochus	yoo-Ril-okus	Persephone	per-Seferni
Eurynome	yoo-Rin-omee	Phoenicia	fa-Nisha
Flora	Flawra	Poseidon	po-Sy-dn
Gaia	Gai-a	Prometheus	pra-Meethus
Glauce	Glaw-see	Psyche	Sy-ki
Hades	Haydees	Raktavija	Ruk-tar-vija
Hathor	Hath-or	Sappho	Safo
Helios	Heeli-os	Sekhmet	Sek-mett
Hephaestus	he-Feestus	Shiva	Sheeva
Hermes	Hermeez	Theseus	Thees-us
Horus	Horus	Tyndareus	tin-Darius
Inanna	In-arna	Zephyrus	Zeferus
Ishtar	Ishta	Zeus	Zoos

FROM GREEK TO ROMAN

The Romans adopted the Greek myths about gods and goddesses, but Latinized some of the names.

GREEK NAME	ROMAN NAME
Aphrodite	Venus
Ares	Mars
Artemis	Diana
Athena	Minerva
Dionysus	Bacchus
Demeter	Ceres
Eros	Cupid
Gaia	Tellus
Hades	Pluto
Helios	Sol
Hephaestus	Vulcan
Hera	Juno
Hermes	Mercury
Odysseus	Ulysses
Poseidon	Neptune
Persephone	Proserpina
Zephyrus	Favonius
Zeus	Jupiter

PICTURE CREDITS

AKG London

page 39 - Diana's Hunt, Zampieri: Rome, Galleria Borghese, © AKG London

page 49 - The Goddess Circe, Dossi: Rome, Galleria Borghese, © AKG London

page 55 - Circe, Allori: Florence, Palazzo Salvati (Banco Toscana), © AKG London

page 74 - Flora's Triumph, Poussin: Paris, Musee du Louvre, © AKG London

page 88 - Isis: Vienna, Kunsthistorisches Museum, © AKG London/Justus Goepel

page 108 - Leda and the Swan, Roman wall painting,: Naples, Museo Nazionale Archeologico, © AKG London/Erich Lessing

page 113 - Medea planning the death of her children: Naples, Museo Nazionale Archeologico, © AKG London/Erich Lessing

page 114 - Medea, vase painting: Paris, Musee du Louvre, © AKG London/Erich Lessing

page 116 - Medea and her children, © AKG London/Erich Lessing

page 119 - Medea kills her children, book illumination: Paris, Bibliotheque Nationale, © AKG London

page 122 - Eva prima Pandora, Cousin: Paris, Musee du Louvre, © AKG London/Erich Lessing

page 132 - Cupid and Psyche, Canova: Paris, Musee du Louvre, © AKG London/Erich Lessing

Ancient Art and Architecture Collection

page 140 - Sekhmet, stone relief

Artephot

page 66 - Grande rilievo da Eleusis, Artephot

page 101 - Kuan Yin, Bronze, Ming dynasty, Artephot/Mandel

page 138 - The Goddess Sekhmet, in black granite, Artephot/Babey

page 143 - Snake Goddess, Artephot/Nimatallah

Australian Picture Library/Bettman Archive
page 43

Australian Picture Library/e.t. archive
10, 11, 15, 33, 42, 65, 71, 72, 89 , 95, 96, 104, 105

Bridgeman Art Library,
page 12 - The Venus of Willendorf, fertility symbol, pre-historic sculpture, 30000–25000 BC (front view), Naturhistorisches Museum, Vienna/Ali Meyer/ Bridgeman Art Library, London,

page 13 - Grey terracotta mother goddess, Mathura, National Museum of India, New Delhi/Bridgeman Art Library, London, London

page 20 - Aphrodite, the 'Venus de Milo', Greek, Hellenistic period, c. 100 BC (marble), Louvre, Paris/Lauros-Giraudon/Bridgeman Art Library, London

page 25 - Minotaur, George Frederick Watts (1817–1904), Tate Gallery, London/ Bridgeman Art Library, London

page 26 - Theseus with Ariadne and Phaedra the daughters of King Minos, 1702 by Benedetto Gennari the Younger (1633–1715), Kunsthistorisches Museum, Vienna/Bridgeman Art Library, London

page 28 - Ariadne at Naxos, Evelyn de Morgan (1855–1919), The De Morgan Foundation, London/Bridgeman Art Library, London

page 30 - Bacchus and Ariadne, Charles Joseph Natoire (1700–1777), Hermitage, St. Petersburg/Bridgeman Art Library, London

page 31 - Bacchus and Ariadne, Sebastiano Ricci (1658–1734), Chiswick House, London/Bridgeman Art Library, London

Cover and page 34 - Diana the Hunter, Orazio Gentileschi (1565–1647), Musee des Beaux-Arts, Nantes/Giraudon/Bridgeman Art Library, London

page 36 - Diana and her followers, lunatics, Parisian copy, c. 1410–15, works of Christine de Pisan (c.1364–1430), British Library, London/Bridgeman Art Library, London

page 38 - Triform Herm of Hecate, marble sculpture, Attic period, 3rd century, Museo Archeologico, Venice/ Bridgeman Art Library, London

page 40 - Athena, statue from Varvakeion, c. 400 BC (marble), National Archaeological Museum, Athens/Bridgeman Art Library, London

page 41 - Minerva, figurine by Girolama Campagna (1549–1625), early 17th century (bronze), Hermitage, St. Petersburg/Bridgeman Art Library, London

page 45 - The Story of Gaia, women in the role of men's work, from 'De Claris Mulieribus', works of Giovanni Boccaccio (1313–1375), Bibliotheque Nationale, Paris/Bridgeman Art Library, London

page 46 - Athena with the Muses, Jacques de Stella (1596–1657), Louvre, Paris/Giraudon/Bridgeman Art Library, London

page 50 - Circe, Giovanni Castiglione (1610–1670), Galleria degli Uffizi, Florence/Bridgeman Art Library, London

page 53 - Circe offering the cup to Ulysses, John William Waterhouse (1849–1917), Oldham Art Gallery, Lancs/Bridgeman Art Library, London

page 57 - Apollo and Daphne, Gerard Hoet (1648–1733), Dulwich Picture Gallery, London/Bridgeman Art Library, London

page 58 - Apollo and Daphne, Paolo Caliari Veronese (1528–1588), San Diego Museum of Art, USA/Bridgeman Art Library, London, gift of Anne R. and Amy Putnam

page 61 - Metamorphosis of Daphne into a laurel tree by Apollo, Charles Sims (1873–1928), The Maas Gallery, London/Bridgeman Art Library, London

page 62 - Demeter, statue from Onidus, Greek, c. 330 BC (marble), British Museum, London/Bridgeman Art Library, London

page 69 - Statue of Ceres, Peter Paul Rubens (1577–1640), Hermitage, St. Petersburg/Bridgeman Art Library, London

SUGGESTED READING

Baring, Anne & Cashford, Jules, *The Myth of the Goddess*, London, Arkana Penguin Books, 1991

Barker, Jennifer & Woolger, Roger, *The Goddess Within*, New York, Fawcett Columbine, 1987

Bolen, Jean, *Goddesses in Everywoman: A New Psychology of Women*, New York, Harper Colophon Books, 1985

Bullfinch, Thomas, *Myths of Greece and Rome*, London, Penguin, 1979

Graves, Robert, *The Greek Myths Vol 1 & 2*, London, Penguin, 1955

Houston, Jean, *The Hero and the Goddess, The Odyssey as Mystery and Initiation*, New York, Ballentine Books, 1992

Monaghan, Patricia, *The Book of Goddesses and Heroines*, Minnesota, Llewellyn Publications, 1993

Richard Aldington & Delano Ames, (trans.) *New Larousse Encyclopedia of Mythology*, London: Hamlyn, 1959

Stone, Merlin, *Ancient Mirrors of Womanhood: a Treasury of Goddess and Heroine Lore From Around the World*, Boston, Beacon Press, 1979

Archeology of the Goddess

Gimbutas, Marija, *Language of the Goddess*, San Francisco: Harper Collins, 1989

Gimbutas, Marija, *Civilization of the Goddess*, San Francisco: Harper Collins, 1991

Index